The Browning of America

The Browning of America

THE HISPANIC REVOLUTION IN THE AMERICAN CHURCH

Isidro Lucas

Fides/Claretian

Printed in the United States of America

ISBN 0-8190-0642-4

Cover design: Glenn Heinlein

Cover art: Ricardo Flores

LC 81-3172

First printing, May 1981

Fides/Claretian books are a series of books, published by the Claretian Fathers and Brothers, which examine the issue of Christian social justice in the United States. The books are written for grassroots Christians seeking social justice. They are based on the premise that it is not possible for everyone to do everything, but it is a Christian duty for everyone to do something.

221 West Madison Street • Chicago. Illinois 60606

To Mary
To John Isidro
To Matthew Francisco

Contents

Foreword   ix

Introduction   1

1. Yo Cuento—No, You Don't   11

2. Geography and National Histories   18

3. A Church That Is Not There   37

4. American Catholics, Hispanic Variety   55

5. Hispanics in the '80s: A New American Leadership   69

6. Who's Picking Up the Slack?   89

7. The Political Future: *Hambre Y Sed de Justicia*   96

8. Empowerment at the Grassroots   107

9. The Language Issue   115

10. Is It a Question of Time?   127

11. A New Doctrine: The Theology of Liberation   133

12. Hispanics Are Here to Stay. Or Are They?   141

Foreword

The Hispanics of the United States are not problems to be solved, nor statistics to be counted, nor objects to be neatly categorized. We are the mystery of the ancient past of the peoples who have inhabited these lands for thousands of years, freely moving back and forth across these vast regions without the interference of humanly-made borders. We are the mystery of the Spanish conquistadores who came to these lands a few hundred years ago and freely mixed with our native ancestors to produce a new race—the cosmic race. We are the mystery of the Latin American *mestizo* who is today undergoing a new *mestizaje* with Anglo-America which will once again produce not merely a new society and a new civilization, but a new race.

As a people, we are very young. The overwhelming presence of youth is evident in every Hispanic community. But it is much more than that, for we are just in the process of being born. The pain and the fascination is that while most racial-cultural groups of people have their origins hidden in their ancient past, we are consciously living and exploring our own birth and growth process.

Sociologists, educators, and census counters become frustrated because we do not fit into their neat categories. We are white, black, and brown; we have black, blue, green, or brown eyes. We are short and we are tall, we are fat and we are skinny. We are rich and we are poor. We are Spanish-speaking and English-speaking. We constantly hear the question, "What do you people want to call yourselves?"

Foreword

We never ask that question ourselves, because we know who we are, but outsiders get frustrated because they cannot define the depth of our mystery.

In our blood, in our minds, in our hearts, and in the very depths of our soul we combine various beautiful cultural traditions and languages. We can truly say, *soy Indio, soy Español, soy Mexicano, soy Estadunidense*. We are a people who have been conquered and oppressed but never fully dominated, for our religion has kept us proud and free. Sure, our church has sometimes oppressed us, but our deeply personal relationship with *Papacito Dios, Jesus, el Nazareno, nuestra madre la Virgen María, y todos los santos* which we have experienced in our homes has given us a deep sense of acceptance and self-worth.

We are a people who have certainly suffered and in many ways continue to suffer. Yet we are not overcome with bitterness or hatred. This does not mean passivity. Precisely because of our deep love for our families and our people, we are struggling, organizing, and taking effective action so as to bring about change in the various structures of society which have oppressed and downgraded our people. The road is not easy, but we will not quit or retreat. The *movimiento* is taking place throughout the country in many diverse ways. We hope to move this country out of its white and English-only self-righteousness.

We are developing our knowledge, a vision of our historical process, organizational techniques, skills, and most of all our own native expressions of our religion. A new people is emerging which is enriching the United States, our Catholic Church, and the Protestant churches as well.

We are not anti-American. Quite the opposite. We believe firmly in the great American dream of liberty and justice for all. What beautiful words: *liberty and justice for all*. Yet, as it is evident from the daily news reports and the pages of this book, for the Hispanic in the U.S. these words have appeared more as hypocrisy than as living truth. Because we believe in a true democracy based on equality, respect, liberty, and justice, we must struggle to bring it about in our homeland. A very high percentage of our Hispanic American men have gone to war and many have received the highest decorations of our country. We are not afraid to fight and die for our country. Our people are very patriotic. Even during the unpopular Vietnam war, our people were never ashamed of their sons and daughters in uniform. We proudly displayed their pictures in uniform in our homes and hung the flag from our houses. Our people have never been ashamed of being loyal and patriotic citizens of this country. The great pain and disappointment is that this has not been reciprocal. In many ways, our country has demonstrated that it has not been proud of us. It has systematically excluded us and continues to degrade us. We have fought and died for the principles of a free and democratic world in Europe and in Asia, and we must do the same within our own country.

Whether we are church-going or not, our people are deeply committed Christians and are not violent. We know that violence is never the road of peace. Violence simply begets greater violence. Yet fight we must; that is our manifest destiny of this century. How? With the weapons of truth, education, demonstrations, the ballot box, marches, neighborhood unions, organization, and, most of all, Christian love. We do not want to destroy what is good and beautiful in the United States, but we no longer want to suffer, or want others to suffer, by what is ugly, hypocritical, or contradictory of the authentic founding principles of this country. In short, we want to struggle so that the United States of America may truly become what it proposes to be: a country wherein every individual person will be treated with dignity and equality.

The best defense against the threats of Marxism is an authentic democracy where the citizens are happy and where they can experience the possibility of betterment. Is it too much to ask America to truly be America? The United States model of democracy loses credibility around the world because people hear about the systematic oppression of the blacks, the Hispanics, the Native Americans. They question whether American-style democracy is not just another fake title for what they are suffering from themselves: powerful oligarchies which oppress the masses of the people and condemn them to a life of perpetual poverty and misery.

The United States can and must become the ray of hope to the rest of the world, but it will not do it through technological, economic, or military supremacy. It will do it by truly living up to what it proclaims itself to be: the land of the free where everyone truly has an equal opportunity. The mission of the oppressed minorities in the United States is to be biblical prophets, or even more, to be like *the* prophet, Jesus of Nazareth, who did not hesitate to go to the wielders of power to proclaim their sinfulness so as to call them to conversion. America was founded by the poor, the oppressed, and the rejected of Europe who risked everything to start a radically new experiment in human living. In fidelity to that same spirit, the oppressed minorities of today must embark on equally heroic ventures so that America will continue to become America. But we must also learn from this noble experiment. Unlike the founding fathers of this country, we do not want to eliminate anyone or displace people from their lands. What we seek is not elimination or exclusion, but the inclusion of everyone. Groups of people are not to be considered as evil, but as gifts of God. The presence of various peoples must be celebrated. All must be able to gather around the banquet table and to enjoy the presence of one another. The new America must be the place where the new Pentecost will be experienced and celebrated: the presence of all the peoples of the world, no longer divided, but united in the joy of each other's presence. Pentecost must become the American feast, but it should not become a hypocritical feast. It must be the joyous celebration of what is just beginning, but is yet to come.

It is a pleasure to introduce this digest-style and easy-to-read book which clearly traces the history, struggles, and aspirations of the Hispanics of the United States. Much has been written on this point, but still the sufferings and goals of our Hispanic peoples continue to be ignored, overlooked, or misunderstood. This book is an excellent contribution for all those who want to understand and appreciate the hidden story of the Hispanics of the United States. We sincerely hope that you will profit from reading this book and pondering the fantastic mystery which these pages help to illuminate.

REV. VIRGIL ELIZONDO
Mexican American Cultural Center

Introduction

In March, 1980, the city of San Antonio, Texas appointed a new chief of police. In San Antonio, Hispanics constitute the majority of the population, but the person appointed chief of police was an Anglo. On the day following the appointment, Patricio Flores, Archbishop of San Antonio, wrote a letter to the mayor and the city council of San Antonio. In it he said, "The failure to appoint Captain Pedro Casillas to the position of chief of police has disappointed many San Antonians, especially the Mexican Americans.... I write to you, our civic leaders, to express our disappointment and concern...."

The reaction from politicians, civic leaders, and the press was vociferous. How did the Archbishop dare to intervene in a matter that concerned only the political domain? Hadn't he heard of the separation of church and state? Criticism from the press was so intense that *El Visitante Dominical,* the national Spanish edition of *Our Sunday Visitor,* published in San Antonio, devoted three of its 12 pages that week to the incident. In its editorial, *El Visitante* made reference to the assassination of Archbishop Oscar Romero, which had taken place a few days before, in El Salvador. Though there is no proportion between one archbishop undergoing martyrdom and another writing a letter, there is at least one small link between the two events: both were examples of a member of the hierarchy espousing the cause of the total welfare of his people.

The minor incident in San Antonio may serve as a point

of departure for this book. A Catholic archbishop had entered the arena of social justice on behalf of Latinos in the United States.

It well may be that the outcry of the San Antonio press and civic leaders was due not only to outrage but to surprise as well. Though in the recent past a number of religious leaders—such as Rev. Martin Luther King, Jr., Rev. Andrew Young, and Rev. Jesse Jackson—have spoken out vigorously for the poor and for social justice, it remains unusual for a Catholic archbishop to speak out publicly on a "secular" issue concerning a minority.

But Archbishop Flores, the first Hispanic to be appointed a bishop in the history of the American church, is an unusual man. Besides his office in the church, he is chairman of the Texas Advisory Committee to the U.S. Commission on Civil Rights. And he is a man of the people, particularly of the Mexican American people.

These people, as well as all the rest of the Hispanics in the United States, are not well known. From time to time newpapers or magazines publish a cover story or a series of articles about the Hispanos, the Latinos, and when they appear the articles are invariably full of talk about "the sleeping giant," the Hispanic people stirring and awakening.

And the Hispanics, though they may be taken for granted, are not well known to the American church either. In May of 1980, Archbishop Robert Sánchez of Santa Fe, New Mexico addressed the National Conference of Catholic Bishops at their semi-annual conference in Chicago. He quoted the Acts of the Apostles (19:2-3) in which Paul, arriving in Ephesus, asks the newly converted if they have received the Holy Spirit. The new believers reply, "We have not even heard that there is a Holy Spirit." Archbishop Sánchez commented: "My brother bishops, let us hope that when we are asked whether we have received among us and served the Hispanics in this country we do not have to answer, 'We did not know that there were Hispanics!' "

Hispanics are assumed to be Catholic and are taken for granted. When Pope John Paul II visited Chicago in 1979 he made a memorable stop at Providence of God Church in Chicago's Mexican American barrio of Pilsen. The people grew hoarse with their endless shouts of "¡Viva el Papa!"

A year later the Archdiocese of Chicago celebrated its 100th anniversary. As the Mayor of Chicago and other dignitaries filed into Holy Name Cathedral, on the opposite side of the street there were 350 uninvited people marching in a quiet demonstration. They were the same people, from the Pilsen neighborhood, who had cheered the Pope. Now they were protesting. In their neighborhood was the abandoned St. Adalbert Convent, empty for five years, which they wanted to buy from the Archdiocese in order to expand a successful day-care center that had a waiting list of 200. They were complaining that they could not get to talk to the Cardinal or anybody on his staff. The organizers of the group said that only intense frustration had been able to overcome their painful reluctance to express themselves in this way against the hierarchy of *their* church.

Not knowing that there are Hispanics, or taking them for granted, may well be a characteristic not only of the country at large, but of the Catholic Church as well. And yet Hispanics, who settled in Florida and the Southwest long before the Mayflower, today make up a substantial proportion of the U.S. population. Their numbers grew from between 9 to 12 million in 1970 to around 14.6 million in 1980, according to preliminary census figures. This does not include 3 million Hispanics living in Puerto Rico. Today, one of every four Roman Catholics in the United States is a Hispanic. In 1978, *Time* dealt with them in a cover story called "The Hispanic Americans." In May of 1980, the *Christian Science Monitor* published a five-part series on Hispanics in the U.S. And the entire July-August 1980 issue of *New Catholic World* was devoted to Hispanic Catholics.

The increase in the numbers of Hispanics, coupled with their increasing awareness of their own characteristics, culture, and needs, warrant the talk of a new "browning of America." This minority can no longer be ignored, for it represents a new and vital force in the United States and in the American Catholic Church.

Hispanics are the new immigrants. Across the Western Plains and into the Midwest, from Texas and California they come—across the 1900-mile border with Mexico; in precarious "freedom flotillas" crossing the straits of the Caribbean from Cuba to Florida; in the first "airborne migration" from the island of Puerto Rico to the large cities of the East and the Midwest. Hispanics today make up the largest group of immigrants settling in this country. For a nation of immigrants, and for a church which must attach profound theological significance to migration and pilgrimage, with their deep biblical implications, this current wave of immigrants is of particular importance.

To know Hispanics better, to learn to communicate with them, to begin to learn from them the special qualities of their culture, so profoundly religious, is a major challenge for all Americans and for all Catholics. This book endeavors to be a primer in this search for knowledge and understanding.

The first question to be taken up is one of name—what to call them. They are known as Hispanics, Latinos, Spanish-speaking, and Hispanos. The U.S. Bureau of the Census prefers to use names derived from specific answers to questions asked in counting this population:

Spanish-speaking is a category that has had a long history in census surveys. It refers to the language spoken in the home as a primary language, the "mother tongue." For more than a century the Census Bureau has identified the various ethnic groups in the population according to their answer to that question.

Spanish origin is an identification which the Census Bureau used for the first time in 1969, relying on the subjective response of all people interviewed to the question of their national origin. In that survey, more than 50 percent of the entire population of the United States gave a specific national origin in response to that question.

Spanish surname is yet another way of identifying this population. In the 1920s, the Immigration and Naturalization Service assembled a list of 8000 Spanish surnames. With modifications, this list is still used by the Census Bureau for identifying persons of Hispanic background. Owing to logistic difficulties in matching names of respondents with names on the list, and to the fact that names of other ethnic origins resemble names on the list, this process is used only in the states of the Southwest.

Certain other names—Spanish ancestry, Spanish descent, and so on—have been used to refer to this population. The terms Latinos, Latin Americans, and Hispanic Americans have been in popular use for years. Currently there seems to be a growing consensus in favor of the term *Hispanic,* particularly in official circles. The Census Bureau first made use of this term, among others, in questionnaires of the 1980 census.

One must bear in mind, however, that all of these are terms of administrative convenience, chosen to group varieties of people and nationalities into some general classifications. The persons thus classified would ordinarily identify themselves differently, according to their specific national origin, in which their historical and cultural roots provide them with a more personal identity than broad census groupings could do.

Thus there are *Mexicans,* often first-generation immigrants from Mexico; Mexican Americans, second-generation immigrants and longer-term Americans; *Chicanos,* who have chosen this once-disparaging name in a defiant assertion of their cultural identity. There are *Puerto Ricans,* both on the island and on the continent. There are *Cubans* and *Cuban Americans;* finally there are Central and South Americans in varying numbers. And there are population groups for whom none of the above names is appropriate—for example, the descendants of the original Spanish settlers, who have been in this territory since before the days of a Mexico or a United States. Some of these people prefer to be called *Hispanos.*

In expressing personal identity and group loyalty, national names always take precedence over administrative classifications. And the names preferred vary from time to time, as peoples' self-awareness and sense of group vary. Name shifts may also take place in order to establish coalitions of several groups to pursue political objectives. It should also be noted that throughout this book the word *Anglo* is used, without prejudice, as a convenient name for the white, non-Hispanic majority.

The great variety of names applied to Hispanic groups should alert the observer to the vast differences that exist among these people. Their histories, their traditions, even their spoken tongues differ. So do the circumstances of their immigration to America. Texans or Hispanos migrate only internally, as do Puerto Ricans coming from the island to the mainland. Mexicans, Cubans, and Central and South Americans have crossed a national border in coming. Some have migrated to escape poverty; others, such as Cubans, have come for political reasons. Knowing these facts will allow the observer to avoid needless stereotyping of Hispanics.

Nevertheless they do have many things in common, most notably the Spanish language. Although there are differences of pronunciation and dialect, all Hispanics share Spanish as a common language—the same language spoken by 300 million people in Europe and the Western Hemisphere. In fact, our Hispanic population makes the United States the fifth-largest Spanish-speaking country in the world.

Another common characteristic is race. Despite their sharing a Spanish European heritage, a large number of Hispanics in America are not sociologically defined as whites. The settlement patterns of the Spaniards, differing from that of the English, has produced in Hispanics a mixed, *mestizo* race, with considerable biological contributions from Native American, and later from African populations.

Introduction

One of the great poets and thinkers of Mexico, José de Vasconcelos, has described this mixture, this *mestizaje,* as a new, *cosmic* race, the only one in which European, African, and Native American stocks have truly mingled, in denial of any racist pretense to "pure" blood, or white supremacy. In a country like America, where race and racial differences have been the cause of so much suffering, and still remain an unsolved problem, this approach of Hispanics to race is revolutionary. It has, in fact, given the word *race* itself a new meaning, so that throughout the whole Spanish-speaking Western Hemisphere, as well as in Spain, Columbus Day is celebrated every year as the *Día de la Raza.* And in this usage *raza* must be translated not as *race* but as *people:* the new cosmic race with its own cultural and historical identity.

Hispanics also have in common the Catholic faith, a fact that will be carefully examined in this book. The meaning of the faith for Hispanics, its permanence in view of migratory and sociological changes, and the impact of religion and of church structures on the Hispanic search for social justice will also be examined.

Hispanics, as a group in America, are poor. The average income of a Mexican American or Puerto Rican is one-third less than that of the majority population. This book is concerned with the poverty and discrimination that Hispanics suffer. The signs once seen in Texas, "No blacks, dogs, or Mexicans" are fortunately gone, but discrimination still persists, as Archbishop Flores had to remind the civic leaders of San Antonio.

Poverty and discrimination form the setting in which to examine the meaning of the church for the growing numbers of Hispanics in America. From a theological viewpoint, the Catholic Church acquires meaning only insofar as it "evangelizes the poor." This basic mission implies some equally basic questions. Does the church in the United States identify itself with these particular poor, the Hispanics, who happen to be Catholic? And as the Hispanics awake to their identity and look for solutions to their socio-political problems, is the church a force moving towards justice, is it an obstacle to social progress, or is it perhaps irrelevant to the entire process?

That is the inquiry of this book. In the search for an answer, both sociological data and theological understandings will be offered, as will opinions and analysis from Hispanic and Anglo leaders, in the church and in the field of social struggle.

Another immediate, relevant question to be examined is to what extent Hispanics, both within and outside the church, are going to have an impact on the American Catholic Church—as well as on America itself. The religiousness and religious practices of Hispanics, as well as the social, political, and educational movements they have created, will necessitate changes in the structure and even in the theology of the church. They will likewise bring changes in the economy and politics of the country.

By the end of the book, it is hoped that the reader will have acquired an initial understanding of this minority, and of its culture and its aspirations. But much will remain unsaid. This book will succeed, perhaps, only to the extent that it will provoke the reader to seek more information, to learn more about Hispanics in America.

At the start of this inquiry a disclaimer is in order. This book is, to a large extent, the log of a personal journey. The facts, when available, are objective; but they may be interpreted in different ways. There is no such thing as an objective evaluation of the thought processes and judgments that take place in the great variety of Hispanic communities. And it would surely make no sense to prescribe a "right" line of thought or action for these Hispanic communities to take. The thoughts and guidelines for action are created every day within these very communities, by their own leaders, by their community organizations, and through the intuition of their poets. From the outside one may only witness, try to understand, and report what is seen to others. But that reporting will not be dispassionate, for the tasks at hand are urgent and there is too little time for their accomplishment.

1

"Yo Cuento"—No, You Don't

In the spring of 1980, many Hispanics in large cities were seen wearing lapel buttons which read "Yo cuento" (I count) and below, the legend, "1980 Census." The buttons were part of the Hispanic communities' campaign to encourage people to respond to the questionnaire of the 1980 Decennial Census: to be counted. These organizations knew the importance of an accurate census count for the future of Hispanics in the United States.

The Decennial Census is the basis for the apportionment of legislative seats at local, state, and federal levels. Legislative districts will be redrawn after the population figures from the 1980 census are in.

Census figures are also the basis for the federal government's revenue-sharing program, the distribution of a portion of the federal tax receipts to state and local governments. It is estimated that for every resident who goes uncounted a city government may lose between $200 and $250 per year of these federal funds. As many as 70 federal aid programs are based on census figures.

The Bureau of the Census spent a billion dollars in its effort to make sure it counted everyone in the 1980 census. Community leaders were deeply concerned to have all Hispanics counted, for many of them had not been counted in the census of 1970. The bureau estimated that it had missed 1.9 percent of the white population and 7.8 percent of the blacks. It could not even make an estimate of the number of Hispanics who had gone uncounted. But in 1974 the U.S. Commission on Civil Rights cited the inaccuracy of the 1970 census in a report called "Counting the Forgotten." Other studies suggested that Hispanics in the Midwest had been undercounted by 20 percent. In some localities the undercount was still higher. In San Jose, California, for example, it was claimed in lawsuits that only 50 percent of the Mexican Americans had been counted.

Sociologists and theologians in Latin America have coined the term "marginated" to describe the plight of the masses of people who live on the margin of a country's economic and political life. It would appear that the term could likewise be applied to the Hispanics in the United States, for in addition to their relative lack of money, jobs, and education, even their numbers are not well known.

Since 1970, the Bureau of the Census has improved its counting process, and for the 1980 census it sought the help of community leaders and organizations to encourage Hispanics to fill out the questionnaires. They decided to solicit help from the Catholic Church as well. In the fall of 1979 the director of the Census Bureau, Vincent Barabba, appeared before the meeting of the U.S. Conference of Catholic Bishops. He and Hispanic leaders suggested that the bishops make a formal statement encouraging Hispanics to be counted and fulfill this civic duty.

The offical regarded this as a noncontroversial matter; nevertheless it proved to be controversial. Many members of Hispanic communities said that responding to the census would expose individuals who were in this country without due residency papers. The bureau responded that such a connection would not be made. Answers to census questionnaires are strictly confidential, and all employees of the Census Bureau are forbidden under criminal penalties to divulge information concerning individuals to anyone, including the Immigration and Naturalization Service.

The American bishops debated the issue, and discussed the possible results of any action they might take. Their final response to the dilemma was a decision to take no action at all. Some of those who had sought a pronouncement respectfully deferred to the decision of their religious leaders, but others were enraged that legal considerations had kept the bishops from a step that would have produced so many benefits for the Hispanics in this country. Some said that if the bishops feared for harm to the undocumented workers they should have taken the active step of dissuading the people, at least the undocumented, from registering. Their lack of action, these critics charged, amounted to the bishops' washing their hands with respect to the fate of the Hispanic people.

Preliminary information on the census in the fall of 1980 pointed to the likelihood that it would once again undercount ethnic and racial minorities, including Hispanics, in the inner cities of America. Suits were filed to remedy the situation in advance. A U.S. District Court in Detroit, in a lawsuit joined by other major cities, decided that an undercount was inevitable, and ordered the Census Bureau to provisionally adjust the initial figures to offset the undercount of blacks and Hispanics. And Congress planned to consider legislation mandating such an adjustment.

The preliminary 1980 census figures indicate an increase of around 60 percent in the Hispanic population since the count of 1970. That represented approximately six times the rate of increase of the total American population. No wonder that there have been claims that Hispanics will constitute the largest minority population in the country by sometime in the 1980s or 1990s.

Moreover, Hispanics are a young population. By 1978 figures, their median age was 22.1 years, compared with 30 years for non-Hispanics. And even without new immigration the Hispanic population will continue to grow as the young people establish new families and enter their child-bearing years.

A popular image of Hispanics in America is that of farm workers, but the fact is that over 85 percent of all Hispanics live in urban areas, mainly in dilapidated housing in the inner cities.

And this population is poor. In 1978 the median income of Hispanic families was $11,421 as compared with $16,284 for non-Hispanic families. Twenty-one percent of Hispanic families had incomes below the poverty level.

Unemployment, another index of economic status, was also greater among Hispanics: 9.5 percent of Hispanics were unemployed, and the figure was even higher among Mexican Americans and Puerto Ricans.

Along with their lower income and higher unemployment goes a lower level of education among Hispanics. Among Hispanic males 25 years of age or older in 1978, nearly 9 percent had only a fifth-grade education or less. Among Hispanic women the figure was over 10 percent. Less than half of the non-Hispanic population of the same age had fared so poorly in education.

And Hispanics fared no better at the upper reaches of the educational spectrum. Only about 9 percent of Hispanic males 25 or older had finished college. Among Hispanic women of that age, only 5 percent had finished college. Of non-Hispanics in the same age group, more than twice as many had completed college.

Figures such as these are dry, but underlying them is a sad picture of poverty and lack of education among Hispanics in the United States. One family out of four lives below the poverty level. Eighty percent of the youths leave high school without a diploma, to join the ranks of the unemployed and unemployable.

The human experience of poverty and alienation that prevails among Hispanics in the United States is the setting in which the role of religion and the organized church among Hispanics needs to be examined.

Although there are no official statistics on the matter, it has been accepted that the majority of Hispanics, both in the United States and in Latin America, are Roman Catholics. Estimates of the number of Catholics among Hispanics run about 85 percent. If the estimates are accurate, Hispanics constitute about 25 percent of all the Catholics in the United States. But what is the relation of these Hispanic Catholics to their church?

The most detailed analysis of the Catholic allegiance of Hispanics in the United States was carried out by the Gallup organization of Princeton University in 1978. There are some problems with the sampling, for it was done by telephone, and a higher than average proportion of Hispanics lack a telephone in their homes. This may be why the Gallup sample shows a higher income for Hispanics than the census figure indicates.

The Gallup survey deals only with Hispanics who identified themselves as Catholic. Far more than half of them responded that for them religion is "very important." But this response varied with the educational level attained by the respondents. Four out of five of those who had completed only grade school considered the church "very important." But of those who had attended college, only 53 percent gave this answer. A similar difference was observed on the scale of income. The higher percentage of those who gave "very important" answers were persons of lower income.

Where actual involvement with the church is concerned, the figures were much lower. Only one in ten of the persons interviewed responded that they are actually working in the church. Yet of those who were doing nothing in the church, more than half responded that they would be interested in giving more time to the church.

From these and other data of the Gallup survey a clear pattern emerges. Hispanics consider themselves Catholic, and for them this fact is important, even though most of them have been the target of zealous proselytizing by other Christian denominations. But in spite of their Catholic allegiance, they have very little active contact with the organized Catholic Church in America.

The outlook for results in church work among Hispanics is good, but the church will have to approach this work with full awareness of their cultural traits, particularly the meaning that the Spanish language has for them. Fifty-six percent of all who responded to the Gallup survey said that in their homes they use Spanish primarily, and another 20 percent said that they use Spanish and English interchangeably. But Spanish is the language they prefer to write and the language they prefer in their home or in their recreation.

As might be expected, more than three-quarters of all

Hispanics desire the church to adapt the liturgy to their needs, with a more thorough use of Spanish as well as other elements of Hispanic culture.

In liturgy the Catholic Church has made remarkable progress, and there is a vital liturgical renewal going on in Hispanic communities across the country.

Language, at one level, is simply a medium for transacting everyday business. For such use the Hispanic is comfortable using either the native or the learned language. But at a deeper level, such as in intimate family relations, even those who are fluent in English prefer the more personal native language. Since religion is personal and familiar among Hispanics, religious experience is best expressed in Spanish. Even among fully bilingual people, few remain bilingual in prayer. Similarly, it is found by professionals in mental health that even the Hispanic person who can communicate in two languages is more comfortable in the native language when expressing intimate aspects of the personality.

The Gallup survey, as well as others that have been conducted in the Southwestern and Northeastern United States, paints a picture of religion among Hispanics that centers on worship, but does not go on to the formation of active religious communities, and which, moreover, is irrelevant to their everyday socio-economic concerns.

The data of surveys and statistics, then, show Hispanics to be a growing minority in the United States, still profoundly immersed in the Catholic tradition, and longing for more vital participation, but taken for granted by the established church. How long their attachment to such a church will continue remains a matter of speculation.

2

Geography and National Histories

It has been said that those who refuse to learn from the errors of history are doomed to repeat them. The warning applies with no less force to those who choose to ignore history.

The Hispanics in the United States have a history, but it is a history that most people ignore. School children in the United States learn about the Pilgrims and other settlers of the Eastern colonies, but their history texts scarcely mention the still earlier settlements of the Spanish in the Southwest and in Florida. And yet the oldest state capitol still standing in the United States is in Santa Fe, New Mexico, founded by the Spaniards in 1610. Even earlier settlements remain, such as El Paso, Texas, founded in 1608, and St. Augustine, Florida, founded in 1593. That early history still affects the lives of Hispanics. It even determines the region in which many of them live. The presence of the Mexican Americans in the Southwest, the immigration of Puerto Ricans to New York, and the settlements of Cubans in Miami all have their roots in a generally ignored history.

History provides special meaning in the search of present-day Mexican Americans for their identity. Even before the "discovery" of the Western hemisphere by the Europeans, the pre-Columbian history of Mexico was unfolding, both in fact and in mythology, in what today is the

Southwest of the United States. The origin of the highly civilized empires of the Mayas, the Toltecs, and the Aztecs is traced to the "land of the North." Legends relate the migration of Nahuatl peoples from *Aztlán*, the land of the North, southward into what is today Mexico. And Aztlán, the center and origin of the pre-European civilization of Mexico, has become the symbol of a new cultural pride, a spiritual fatherland for the nationalist movement which has adopted the name *Chicano*.

The Southwest

What is now New Mexico began with the explorations of the Franciscan Father Marcos de Niza in 1539. He and his companions were searching for the Seven Cities of Cibola and their rumored fabulous riches. In 1595, Juan de Oñate began settling New Mexico, and years later his successor founded Santa Fe.

The territory of Florida was first explored by the ill-fated expedition of Pánfilo de Narváez. And the original exploration of California was carried out in the 1540s by Juan Rodríguez Cabrillo.

The colonizing methods of the Spanish differed greatly from those of the English, in the East. The Spanish king and the church were bound together, and an imperial purpose went side by side with a missionary spirit. The crown viewed the task of conquest and settlement as a divine mission to incorporate the peoples and their territories, not only into Christendom but also into the Spanish empire. The lofty vision did not deter the crown or its representatives from the profit seeking which spurred the conquests on. The missionaries, first led by Father

19

Bartolomé de las Casas, strongly condemned the Spanish abuse of Native Americans in the conquered territories. Their critical voice remained strong throughout the Spanish colonial period.

The history of the Spanish colonies comes, in most cases, from two parallel sets of documentation: one from the governors, military leaders, and entrepreneurs, the other from the missionaries. Each group sought the king's ear to complain of the actions and abuses of the other group.

In few places is the connection of religious and secular rule more evident than in the settlement of California. The dominant Spanish influence is found in the unique institution of the *Mission*. The first of these was established by Father Junipero Serra at San Diego. The work was encouraged by the crown, which hoped thereby to prevent an expansion of Russian explorations from Alaska southward. All together, Father Serra established 21 missions along the California coast. Among them was *El Pueblo de Nuestra Reina de Los Angeles,* now the city of Los Angeles, founded in 1781.

There are still reminders of these missions in the mission churches, many of which are still in use. The missions were an experiment in adapting the Native Americans to the ways of the Spanish settlers. They were communal towns, ruled by the missionaries and exempt from secular authority. They attempted to teach the Indians first religion, but simultaneously European civilization, trades, agriculture, and crafts. The character of the missions was paternal authoritarianism, often tempered with benevolence.

Around 1830, the missions were abolished by the new independent government of Mexico. The same thing happened throughout the Spanish-speaking world around that time. And the subsequent abuse of the Indians by the secular authorities and profiteers surpassed the injustices of the padres.

The fathers of Mexican independence were two Catholic priests: Father Miguel Hidalgo, the curate of Dolores, and following the defeat and execution of Father Hidalgo, in 1811, Father José María Morelos, of Morelia. Hidalgo's rebellion is still commemorated as the beginning of Mexico as a nation.

But by and large the Catholic Church remained faithful to the king and to Spain at the time of the wars of independence. This is easier to understand when one considers that the revolution that swept the Spanish colonies beginning in 1810 was more than a territorial and political revolt. It embraced a revolutionary ideology. It called for the end of the "divine right" monarchy and to the close relationship between the secular and religious authority. It proposed a secular government, based on democratic principles, which justified its power not on divine right but on the consent of the governed. These ideas, born in the French Enlightenment, and tested briefly in the French Revolution, lay behind the American Revolution, too, and the Constitution that followed it. But they were frightening to the Spanish clergy of the colonies.

Some historians assert that even after the Spanish colonies had become independent nations, the church structures remained colonial in outlook, as well as in the nationality of the clergy, which even today is made up mainly of Spanish-born priests. This theory might explain the aloofness of the organized church from the popular social and political movements in Latin America since independence.

The Browning of America

In the outlying Spanish territories of the present American Southwest, the new government of Mexico was received with little hesitation, though here and there some were reluctant to swear off allegiance to the old crown.

Even before independence, the Spanish government became worried over the sparse population it had been able to attract to the large part of Mexico that is now Texas. Thus the government began to accept non-Spanish settlers in Texas. This began with the land grant made to Moses Austin in 1821. In 1823, the new Mexican government was in power and renewed the grant, with the conditions that the settlers pledge their allegiance to the Mexican authorities, that they restrict the number of families to be settled, and that the families either be Catholic, or planning to become Catholic. By 1829, the Mexican government had made up to 20 land grants to American settlers, with similar conditions.

These American settlers in Texas were caught between the demands of a distant and unstabilized government in Mexico City and their own local needs and political aspirations. Restless under orders of the central government, the American settlers in Texas rebelled. After fighting Mexican forces in the battles of the Alamo and San Jacinto, Texas declared itself independent. The new Republic of Texas was declared in 1836, and it immediately requested to be annexed to the United States.

The territorial philosophy of the United States at the time was that of "Manifest Destiny." In 1845, the U.S. Congress accepted the offer of Texas to be annexed, but the price it had to pay was the war with Mexico. In the treaty that concluded that war, the defeated Mexico yielded all five of the present states of the Southwest to the United States.

The Treaty of Guadalupe Hidalgo has not been thoroughly studied by historians. As originally drawn it included an Article X, guaranteeing the land grants in the newly acquired territories, with specific mention of grants made to the church and church institutions. But before ratifying the treaty Congress struck out that article and referred instead to the section of the documents of the Louisiana Purchase which guaranteed religious rights, but in less detail.

The new treaty provided that the residents of those former Mexican territories would have one year to choose between American and Mexican citizenship. Only about 200 people chose to move to Mexico.

A year after the signing of the Treaty of Guadalupe Hidalgo gold was discovered in California, and the vast migration of Americans left the formerly predominant Mexicans in a minority status. The history of relationships between Hispanics and Anglos in the Southwest is complex, and differs from region to region. New Mexico long remained unchanged, by and large; it did not even become a state until 1912.

In Texas there was strong animosity and strife between Americans and Mexicans. In California, economic forces gave Americans the dominant social and political role, reducing the Mexicans to a minority status. The history includes both deprivation of land and mutual violence, in which the activity of Mexican bandits figured. In Texas and California, lynching was introduced for the first time, and its victims were Mexicans. There were also political abuses, such as the importing of peons to cast fraudulent votes in elections. And the Mexican population suffered more and more discrimination, especially in Texas, but also in California, and to a lesser extent in New Mexico.

The clash between Mexicans and Americans had implications for the organized Catholic Church. The stereotype of the Mexicans as a lazy and uncultured people was applied even to the native clergy who remained in the new territories. From highest levels the church undertook a new "evangelization" of the area, and sent French and Belgian priests and bishops to reorganize the church. There were many confrontations between the newly arrived missionaries and the original Spanish-speaking clergy of the Southwest. At times there were stormy efforts to replace the local parish clergy. Here and there the clash reached levels that some have labeled ecclesiastical schism. The church had to resolve, in practice, the question of whether its mission was primarily to evangelize or to Americanize the people. Many will say that that dilemma has still not been resolved.

The Hispanics of the Southwest became American citizens without taking the usual step of migrating here. But it took a long time before the U.S.-Mexican border became an effective cultural and political boundary. The nearly 1900-mile border is a human construction, incorporating no physical barriers. For many years two-way passage of the border took place every day, and migration between the two countries was a way of life.

There have been several waves of migration from Mexico to the United States, generally the results of changing political and economic conditions. Only in the second third of this century did the inequalites of the two economies make migration to the U.S. a powerful attraction to many Mexicans.

The first big immigration occurred in the 1910s, when Mexico was in the throes of a major revolution and thousands of refugees sought shelter across the border. Most of the later waves of migration were motivated by economic betterment. A scarcity of workers during the First World War led to recruitment of workers in Mexico by large agriculture and major heavy industries. From the 1910s and 1920s on, the destinations of immigrants were no longer confined to the Southwest; they began to settle in the Midwestern and Western states as well. The first Catholic parish for Mexicans in Chicago, Our Lady of Guadalupe, was founded in 1924 and still serves Mexican Americans.

In the 1920s, a new U.S. immigration policy was taking shape, and its main concerns were to limit total immigration and to give preference to certain countries of origin. During the '30s, the depression years, the federal government encouraged and even forced the return of many Mexican immigrants to Mexico. Welfare officials found the repatriation of Mexicans cheaper than carrying them on public assistance, and during the '30s trains full of Mexicans left California and the Midwest for the Mexican border. In Chicago alone, the Mexican population was reduced by almost 50 percent. Incomplete studies have claimed that as many as a quarter of the repatriated Mexicans were American-born.

There was a new wave of immigration from Mexico in the '40s, once again spurred by a scarcity of workers in wartime. And at this time there was a new form of migration: that of the temporary seasonal farmworker, the *bracero*.

During the '50s a new phenomenon occurred: that of entry into the U.S. from Mexico without proper credentials—the "illegal alien" or undocumented worker. The political problem of this phenomenon still remains unsolved, and the issue is very sensitive for all Hispanics. This immigration is still going on, and the future course of it is not easy to predict. The population of Mexico is growing faster than its economy, so immigration to the U.S. is attractive to the unemployed and eager-to-work population.

Popes and bishops of the Catholic Church have expressed themselves forthrightly on the issue of immigrants, and they make no fundamental distinction between legal and undocumented immigrants. It is firmly rooted in Christian teaching that the church is a pilgrim on earth, and as such it has a natural empathy with those who are still in the midst of the migration process. Hispanics literally fulfill that description, whether they come from Mexico, from Puerto Rico, or from other Latin American countries.

Puerto Ricans: The Airborne Migration

Borinquén, strategically situated in the Caribbean Sea, was first visited by Columbus in 1504. Its original inhabitants, the Tainos and Arawacs, disappeared as an identifiable people within the first 75 years of Spanish colonization, owing to the harsh conditions of the conquest and settlement and to intermarriages with Spaniards.

Since its scanty resources of gold and silver were soon exhausted, it was difficult for the Spanish crown to attract enough settlers to the island. Thus it remained chiefly a military post, guarding the entrance to the Caribbean from military and merchant ships. Puerto Rico, as the Spanish called it, was the scene of many military encounters. El Morro castle still stands in San Juan, a remainder of the fortifications the Spaniards built to protect the island and the rest of the Spanish colonies from Dutch, French, and English privateers.

When the mainland Spanish colonies fought and won their wars of independence, Puerto Rico and Cuba remained unaffected. Indeed, many of the loyalists fleeing from the other colonies took refuge in Puerto Rico; many say that this conservative element was a major cause of the delay in the liberation movements in Puerto Rico. As the winds of independence continued to blow over the island there was a solid class of merchants and wealthy landowners, calling themselves *incondicionales* (unconditionals), who pledged an unquestioned allegiance to the Spanish government. The clergy, most notably the upper hierarchy, consistently sided with this group.

Among the people who did seek a major change there were two main groups: the *independentists* and the *autonomists*. The independists were opposed to any form of colonial status. Some of them were in exile, especially in New York, helping to plot the liberation of the island. They got so far as to send a ship to aid the uprising in Lares, on the island. But the ship was detained by American forces at St. Thomas in the Virgin Islands, and did not reach Puerto Rico in time to aid the rebellion.

The other group seeking a change in Puerto Rico's

27

status favored autonomy. They sought concessions from the Spanish government which would provide a measure of self-determination within the framework of the Spanish government. And the autonomists achieved a certain success, at least on paper, when the Spanish government issued the charter of 1897, giving Puerto Ricans the right to elect a local legislative body and to adopt their own budget, subject to the final approval of the Spanish Cortes, as well as to negotiate trade with foreign countries.

But the charter never took effect. For in the meantime, following the dubious incident of the sinking of the battleship *Maine,* the United States took up the cause of the Cuban revolution and declared war on Spain. This war, fought not only in the Caribbean but in the Philippines as well, ended in victory for the United States.

The United States had made a landing on Puerto Rico as well, and the Spanish forces surrendered after token resistance. The Puerto Ricans gave the Americans a joyful reception.

At the treaty of Paris, which formally ended the Spanish American War, Spain ceded Puerto Rico to the United States. Some Puerto Ricans have maintained that Spain had no right to give away an island it no longer possessed, since it had granted virtual independence to that territory.

At first, American military governors ruled Puerto Rico, but later the President of the United States appointed civilian governors. A new legal structure for the government was established by the Foraker Act of 1903. This was modified by the Jones Act of 1917, by which Puerto Ricans were made citizens of the United States.

During and after World War II, Luis Muñoz Marín secured a new status for Puerto Rico: that of Commonwealth or *Estado Libre Asociado* (Free Associated State). This provision deferred the issue of a permanent status for the island, which remains a major political concern. Puerto Ricans now elect their governor, their representatives in the legislature, and a commissioner who represents them in the U.S. House of Representatives. The Puerto Rican commissioner sits in the House and works as a full member on committees but does not have a vote in the decisions of the House.

When Puerto Rico became a Commonwealth, Muñoz Marin, together with the New Deal, undertook programs to convert Puerto Rico from a mainly agricultural economy to a flourishing industrial economy. This program was dubbed Operation Bootstrap in English and *Operación Manos a la Obra* in Spanish. It provided for land reform, for large tax concessions to newly established business and industry, and for a major effort to train and educate the Puerto Rican workforce.

Operation Bootstrap worked well at first, though to this day most of the land is still used for large-scale agriculture, chiefly sugar production. Many industries were attracted to the island, and Puerto Ricans achieved the highest per capita income among all the Latin American countries. But the slowdown of the American economy has had a disastrous effect on Puerto Rico. It is estimated that the rate of unemployment there is now close to 20 percent. Moreover, many of the industries that had begun in Puerto Rico have either moved away in search of cheaper labor, or have reorganized under new names to secure the tax benefits granted to new industries.

An apparently intentional consequence of Operation Bootstrap was the effort to export the surplus of workers on the island. The circumstances of World War II, followed by the boom of the U.S. economy in the '50s and the '60s, accelerated this movement of workers, and the airborne migration began. The destination was the Northeastern United States. Workers were needed in the large food and garment industries of New York, and at first there was a demand for harvest workers in the Northeastern states. The migration continued until 1972, at which time a net return migration to Puerto Rico was first detected. The reverse movement went on until 1978. Lately there are signs that migration is flowing again towards the continent. Precise data are hard to get because this migration is internal, and does not pass any official checkpoint.

The Catholic Church has not been committed to any political policies concerning Puerto Rico, but after the U.S. acquired the island its hierarchy became an integral part of the U.S. episcopate, and the island received many Irish and other English-speaking missionaries. Historically, the position of the leadership of the Catholic bishops of Puerto Rico has been politically conservative. Before the Charter of 1897, the Archbishop of San Juan, sitting in the Spanish Cortes, encouraged the government to reinstitute slavery in Puerto Rico, from which it had long been banished, arguing that the many Negroes would be better off and happier under the protection of a master. For many years, even in the 20th century, the church in Puerto Rico would not ordain black candidates to the priesthood, because "the people would not want to receive communion from the hands of a Negro."

In the last few years, however, under the influence of movements in Latin America, there has been a growing concern for social justice in the Puerto Rican church. Some of the Catholic groups which have been formed have adopted socialist doctrines and are committed to social change. The voice of Bishop Antulio Parrilla Bonilla, a Jesuit, has joined those of the many proponents of a liberation theology, in which social commitment and the cause of the poor will take a leading role in a revitalized church.

On the continent, Puerto Ricans are now concentrated in New York and along the Eastern Seaboard, but they also extend into western Pennsylvania, Ohio, Michigan, Illinois, and Wisconsin, chiefly in the major industrial cities.

The Cuban Exile

Cubans, unlike Mexican Americans and Puerto Ricans, have immigrated to the U.S. as a result of a single political event. There had been some Cubans in America, but it was the rise of Fidel Castro to power, January 1, 1959 that prompted the huge influx of Cubans that is still going on.

There have been several stages in the exodus of the Cubans. In the first few months of the Castro regime, the wealthier entrepreneurs and industrialists left the country. Later, professionals and lower-middle-class people left for America. But relations between America and Cuba hit bottom after the Bay of Pigs invasion and the missile crisis of 1962. Cuba tightened its exit policies and legal immigration to the U.S. became almost impossible.

Then, in 1965, Cuba and the United States reached an agreement for the orderly exit of Cubans to the U.S. The United States wanted to prevent loss of life, and the Cuban government wanted to arrange for the exile of dissidents from the revolutionary regime. The airport of Varadero, Cuba became the point of departure for the popular

"freedom flights" which brough to Florida a large group
of Cubans, made up of the lower-middle-class, workers in
skilled trades, and even manual laborers.

These several waves of the Cuban immigration constituted the great bulk of the movement up until 1980. The
federal government established a special Cuban refugee
program which provided money for relocation, retraining,
and re-education. Many Americans opened their homes
and their churches to the newcomers. It was perhaps the
last major effort of the country in the spirit of the cold war,
when political and ideological lines between communism
and the "free world" were clearly drawn and were accepted.

Their rather high level of education enabled many Cubans to step into positions such as teaching and social service. In 1965, Congress passed the initial Bilingual Education Act, largely because of empathy with the newly-
arrived Cubans. The first large and successful bilingual
education program was established in Dade County,
Florida.

The Catholic Church in Cuba had been caught unaware
by the Castro revolution. The hierarchy had been conscious of the social and economic abuses of the Batista
regime, but had not adopted a policy of speaking out
against them. As the militia accompanying Castro from
the mountains made victorious entries into the towns and
cities they ostentatiously displayed crosses and religious
medals over their uniforms. But as the relationship between Castro and the United States declined, Cuba declared itself a communist country. In 1962, without warning, the Castro government rounded up as many as 150

bishops, priests, and nuns, and put them on a Spanish ship bound for Spain.

Today, however, the church is present and active in Cuba. The old stereotype of communism as all that is atheistic and anti-Christian has given way to an objective appraisal of life under the revolutionary regime. Seminarians, who are few but highly motivated, periodically undertake the kind of manual work the regime demands of all students and white-collar workers. Insofar as the revolution has improved conditions for the lowest economic classes and proclaims political goals of social justice, the Cuban church is in agreement. But the controlled conditions of life in Cuba do not permit an observer to predict the role and the future of the church under a communist regime with whose doctrine and methods it must continue to disagree.

The popular assumption in the United States today is that the Cubans have made a successful transition from their native language and former occupations in the 20 years since the Cubans began to settle in Miami, as well as in other large cities. In Miami they have not only altered the traits of the city but have also promoted a new prosperity through their export-import businesses, thus making Miami the center of American trade with Latin America. Cuban pupils learn well in schools. The incomes of Cubans are still below the national average, but are steadily approaching it.

Nevertheless, there has been a high dropout rate among Cuban students in Miami, and many Cubans, like other immigrants, find difficulty in adapting to life in a foreign country. Family incomes are higher because a high proportion of Cuban women, too, are employed. One of the major social problems is that there are many elderly persons among them who have difficulty learning English and acquiring the social skills necessary for entering the American mainstream. And many of the older people lack the credits needed for Social Security assistance. Their poverty and isolation are depicted regularly in horror stories in the newspapers.

In 1980, there came a new, frantic wave of Cuban immigration. When it was over, as suddenly as it had started, between 125,000 and 150,000 Cubans had arrived in the United States. The new exiles have come for economic as well as political reasons. They belong to poorer economic classes and are more mixed in racial composition than the earlier immigrants were. Their reception has been less cordial than that accorded to those who came before. Many of them seem to have been forced to leave Cuba, to further certain political goals of the Castro government.

After initial hesitation, a great number of the Cubans have acquired American citizenship. Many of them lean to the right in politics; any prospect of drastic social change reminds them of the Cuban revolution, which also proclaimed social justice but resulted in a dictatorship. Nevertheless some Cubans have leagued themselves with other Hispanics in the struggle for equality.

In religious practices, too, Cubans lean toward traditional ways which to many would appear to be conservative. Still, there is no solid Cuban bloc. In the last few years a closer relationship has developed between Cuban and other Hispanic groups in relation to religious and church matters. Cuban priests as well as laity take part in

Hispanic "encounters." And Cubans are embracing the revival of a liturgy of definite Hispanic character. Likewise, Cuban church leaders have joined the rest of the Hispanics in the Hispanic Secretariat of the Conference of Catholic Bishops.

Other Hispanic Groups

Immigrants from the many Latin American countries have been coming to the United States for a number of years. One reason has been the political upheavals in many Latin American republics; another has been the desire for better economic opportunity. Scattered surveys of the income and education of these immigrants shows them to be an extremely diverse group, ranging from the uneducated laborer to the highly trained professional.

During the past 20 years there has been some illegal immigration from several Latin American countries. It is said, for example, that there may be up to 400,000 immigrants without proper residency papers in and around New York City. But there is very little information available on the matter.

Immigrants from Latin America also vary in respect to their association with the major Hispanic groups in the United States. Seeing that Hispanics in this country are regarded as an ethno-racial minority, many of the Latin American immigrants, particularly those with higher education and incomes, choose not to identify themselves with Hispanics. They aim, instead, at being assimilated into the general American population, as other immigrants before them have done. On the other hand, they do join social groups of their own compatriots in which they can maintain emotional and cultural ties with their native country. And yet there are Latin American immigrants who do join the other Hispanics in the United States in dealing with the issues that face them in their struggle for social progress.

3

A Church That Is Not There

When the 96th Congress of the U.S. met in 1978 its membership included four Hispanics in the House (five counting the nonvoting Commissioner of Puerto Rico) but no Hispanic senator. Had Hispanic citizens been represented according to their proportion in the population, there would have been more than 20 Hispanics in the House of Representatives. No less distressing is the lack of Hispanic representation in all other elective offices, both at state and local levels. The same holds true for Hispanic employment in federal civil service. Even after four years of special programs of affirmative action, Hispanic representation remains less than 4 percent.

The phenomenon of margination, defined earlier, is apparent in the status of Hispanics in the political realm. Their lack of participation in power structures has led Hispanics, as well as other minorities, to demand affirmative action to remedy the inequities they suffer in employment and education.

If Hispanics feel left out in secular society, they feel no less left out in the church, which leads to a sense of alienation. The Chicano poet Luis Valdés, an associate of César Chávez in the farmworkers' struggle, was recently asked what part the church had played in the struggle. His answer was blunt and maybe not quite accurate. What he said was: "The church was not there."

At another time, a prominent Puerto Rican educator in New York City was interviewed on the subject of the church's involvement in the struggle of the Puerto Ricans for justice and equality. He said emphatically that the church as an organization was not taking the part of this minority—indeed, that the leadership of the church was aligned with the power structures and was not using its political influence in favor of the Hispanics. When the interviewer remarked that he seemed to be bitter, he replied, "I *am* bitter. After all, it is *my* church. It's painful to see it uninvolved."

The alienation and bitterness of Hispanics towards the church sometimes results in direct confrontation. A dozen years ago, while the Cardinal Archbishop of Los Angeles was building the new Church of St. Basil, he was faced several times by a group of militant Hispanics, protesting the great expenditure for the church and requesting funds for the needs of Hispanic Catholics. The Cardinal said that the church had already done a great deal for Hispanics, and that the archdiocese had no money for the programs that this group, *Católicos por La Raza*, were sponsoring.

On Christmas eve of 1969, the church was dedicated, the Cardinal himself celebrating the Mass. Outside, on the church steps, the *Católicos* group had organized a Spanish Mass. When the Chicanos attempted to enter the church by the main doors, they found them closed. Then they tried to get in through the side doors. What followed was more like the clashes of protestors at government sites than an assembly of Catholics with their leaders. A large number of police attempted to disperse the demonstrators. More than 20 people were arrested, and a number of persons were injured. This incident had a deep effect on the *Católicos,* and its repercussions were felt throughout the country, even though the Anglo press gave it only scanty coverage. What was at stake in the confrontation, according to one of the leaders of the *Católicos,* was the Hispanics' vision of the church as acting in their behalf, as their "hope-maker." When the church limits its action for the poor to the distribution of Christmas and Easter food baskets, or to missions for the derelict, the frustration of the Hispanic people and their leaders is great, because their capacity for hope in the church is great, and such hope unfulfilled causes great frustration.

The alienation of Hispanics from church structures is shown both in public demonstrations and in quiet expressions of despair in the church's leadership. A source of this despair is the low representation of Hispanics in the hierarchy of the church. Of the 360 bishops in the American Catholic Church, only 12 are Hispanic, and fewer than half of these are heads of dioceses.

There were no Hispanic bishops at all in the American church until 1970, when Father Patricio Flores was consecrated bishop to be an auxiliary for the diocese of San Antonio, Texas. He is now Archbishop of San Antonio.

There is not only a lack of Hispanic bishops, but also a lack of Hispanic priests. Father Angelico Chávez, O. F. M., said in 1975 that so far as he could ascertain, and he is a historian, he was the first Mexican American in the United States to have been ordained a Franciscan priest.

The best analysis of Hispanics and the priesthood in America has been done by Father Rutilio del Riego, a Spaniard who has worked for several years in San Antonio, in Washington, D.C., and now in New York, with the Hispanic Pastoral Center for the Northeast. His latest survey shows that there are 1415 Hispanic priests in the

United States, which is 2.4 percent of the priests in this country. More than half of these are members of religious orders. One-third of these priests are American born, another third are from Spain, and the rest were born in Latin America.

There are also many American priests who have learned Spanish and use it in pastoral ministry to Hispanics. There are other priests who, even without knowing Spanish, are able to reach Hispanic congregations through a special sensitivity to them and through their growing appreciation of Hispanic culture. The ministry of these priests is highly effective in creating a church of believers.

But the fact that there are only 400 native-born Hispanic priests—so few in proportion to the Hispanic population— seriously affects the relationship of the Hispanics with the church in America. Critics have called this church too Irish; be that as it may, it is too little Hispanic. Religious ministry to other nationalities has been helped by the church's incorporation of their own ethnicity and culture. But by and large the church has been unable to do the same in ministering to Hispanics.

Groups of European immigrants have produced a good number of priests and bishops of their own nationality. Among Hispanics this has not occurred. There have been no major studies to explain this lack, though there are hypotheses.

One of the reasons offered is historical: in the tradition of the Latin American church there seems to have been a long-standing gap, in both social class and psychology, between the clergy and the people. The priests were mostly Spanish, and their attitude toward the faithful colonial. It is suggested that a similar attitude prevailed among American clergy in their relationship with Hispanics.

But such class distinctions are an insufficient explanation, for in other countries peasant and working-class candidates for the priesthood are drawn into the middle class through the long secular and religious process of the formation of priests in the Catholic Church. Social commentators in Europe have claimed that priestly "vocations" have been one avenue for the social aspirations of the poor. But such a phenomenon, even if proved, did not occur in Latin America, nor has it occurred in the United States with respect to Hispanics.

When one asks Hispanic bishops in the U.S. why there is such a scarcity of Hispanic priests, some of them say, "It's the church's fault," and point out that there has been no concerted effort to attract Hispanics to the priesthood. One bishop bluntly said, "Have you visited our seminaries? Have you as a Catholic had any contact with our Hispanic clergy? What are we offering our young Hispanic people? The church is just not interested in them."

Awareness of this problem, and a sense of collective guilt for it, was not present among a group of Anglo bishops when they were asked about Hispanic vocations. A Cardinal who is in charge of one of the largest archdioceses admitted that there were hardly any Hispanic vocations. When asked for the reason he said he thought it was a part of the general decline of vocations in the church. Worldly temptations were luring the youth of every group away from dedicating themselves to the ministry. Then someone asked him why there had been so few Hispanic aspirants even in days of plentiful vocations. His answer was simple: he did not know.

In searching for an answer, one comes back to the fact that it requires a certain level of education to be admitted to the seminary and remain in it. But data show that Hispanics do not do well in U.S. schools, and that they are less well educated than the general population.

But that in itself raises questions that go to the core of the values currently embraced by the church in America, and perhaps in the whole world. Which is more important: to have priests with a high level of education—the sign of the middle-class background—or to have priests with a strong religious commitment which would enable them to minister to the needs of people of their own background? In theory there need be no conflict between a high level of education and a strong religious commitment. But historically the church seems to have waited for a social class to rise before accepting its members for ministerial service.

Another explanation given for the lack of Hispanic candidates for the priesthood is one of the demands that the church makes of its clergy, namely celibacy. The question is pointed, because there is no serious theological claim that celibacy is essential to the priesthood, despite statements sometimes made by less-informed Catholic leaders, even in the hierarchy. Celibacy is merely a requirement of ecclesiastical discipline, and one that church authorities could remove without any implications for dogma.

The notion that celibacy explains the absence of Hispanics from the priesthood carries weight with many, because of the stereotypes of "Latin blood" and machismo which are thought to characterize the Hispanic male.

If Hispanics have difficulty with celibacy it is at levels much deeper than this stereotype. When well-informed Hispanic Catholics discuss this issue, they say that it is not the renunciation of "the joys of the flesh" that dissuades Hispanic youth from priestly celibacy. It is rather that celibacy severs the ties that these young Hispanics have, and hope to create, with a family and a community.

Training for the priesthood and celibacy radically alters these ties. Residential seminaries, traditionally, have done their best to create a separate, isolated group of men who will be adapted to fulfill the role of a pastoral ministry untouched by family and social linkage, as befits the celibate priest. Those who are familiar with the strong family and community ties that are inherent in Hispanic culture realize that this isolation and detachment are contradictory to that culture.

The present Vicar General of a diocese in the Southwest, a Chicano, recalls an experience of his own. While he was in the seminary word reached him from home that his uncle was dying. When he asked for permission to go to see him he was at first refused. An uncle was not a member of the immediate family, so any such permission would have to be considered by the highest authority in the seminary. This was done, and ultimately the permission was granted. What the professors at the seminary did not know, the Vicar General adds, is that he was resolved to go to visit his dying uncle with or without permission, regardless of whether it would cause his expulsion from the seminary. Though the sick man was "only" an uncle, to this young man, bound to his family, he was too important a person not to rush to his deathbed.

It may be a truism to say it, but as long as there is no "native" clergy Hispanic Catholics will never be fully incorporated in the church in the United States. This fact is confirmed by the yearning of the Hispanic faithful to have their own priests.

In the 1978 Gallup survey on the church attendance of Hispanics, respondents were asked why they thought there were so few Hispanic priests. One-fifth answered, "discrimination" but more than three-quarters of the respondents, all Catholics, expressed their desire that there should be more Hispanic priests. Of the respondents having only a grade-school education, 82 percent said they would like to see more Hispanic priests. To the survey question on whether they would encourage their sons or daughters to go into the priesthood or religious life, a majority replied that they would. Such responses give a glimpse of the religious commitment of the Hispanic faithful, in spite of the obstacles of church regulations and socio-economic barriers.

This commitment may be the explanation of what seems to be a more hopeful outlook for the ordination of Hispanic priests, for despite the general decrease in candidates for the priesthood in the U.S. today, there seems to be an increase of Hispanic candidates. At present, according to the research of Father Rutilio del Riego, over 6 percent of the seminarians in the U.S. today are Hispanics; at the high-school level of seminary preparation nearly 9 percent of the candidates are Hispanic.

There may be sociological as well as theological reasons for this apparent upward trend. Perhaps the newly acquired consciousness concerning Hispanics in the North American church has begun to take effect. It has given rise to regional seminaries and to seminaries specifically for Hispanics. In a statement of simple faith, a bishop said, "Vocations have to be there. God would not do otherwise than to provide these vocations. It is up to us to find and foster them."

Along with this new consciousness, there may also be another phenomenon at work. For while there is a decrease of candidates for the priesthood in the so-called developed countries, there appears to be an increase in the

A Church That Is Not There

"under-developed" or developing countries. This has been seen in various Latin American and African countries. And in those countries the increase in vocations has come hand in hand with a reorientation of the church, with a renewed commitment to serving the poor. This new trend is not a fad; it is a rediscovery of the deepest meaning of Christian life. It had its origins in a specific awareness of class, which was expressed in a dedication to the classes ranked lower in social and economic standing. Their spiritual and material needs determined the church's preference to place these classes first. Hispanics, as they re-emphasize this old-new commitment and make it the center of their theology, may be lighting the way toward a new revival for the rest of the American church.

Discrimination, one hopes, is disappearing from the Catholic Church in America. Gone, in the Southwest, are the separate cemeteries for Anglos and Mexican Americans. Gone are church services for Mexicans only, offered as a compensation and as a practical way of barring them from "regular" services. For that matter, gone, too, are the special black missions within walking distance from white Catholic parish churches.

In the future, Hispanic Catholics may take the role of leading the American Catholic Church in this way of tradition. If so, they will no longer be just a tolerated class in the church, but pioneers blazing the trail back to its original mission.

Many Hispanic church leaders are already claiming such a role. In discussing the issue of married priests, for example, they are fully aware of the important pastoral reasons favoring a change in the discipline of celibacy for the American and worldwide Catholic Church, but they insist that they want no exception made for the Hispanic church alone. The change, if needed, should be made for the entire church, but they do not want a Hispanic clergy of a second class, who would never be eligible for the hierarchy of the church, as occurs in the Eastern churches, where married men may be ordained, but cannot be made bishops.

There is a new awareness and a new optimism among Hispanics about their role in the functioning and organization of the church, even though they would like to see changes made. One sign of this optimism is the Hispanics' acceptance of the reinstated function of the "permanent" diaconate in the American church.

For the moment there seems to be a pause taking place for reflection upon and analysis of the manner of preparation of candidates for the diaconate, whether married or not. The pace of entry into this ministry has at least temporarily decreased. For 1980 however, a reliable source placed the count of "permanent" deacons in American dioceses at 4093. More than 10 percent of these, it appears, are Hispanic.

Such Hispanic participation calls for reflection. As for the hierarchy, many Anglo bishops see the Hispanic deacons as a blessing for them in their ministry to the Hispanic faithful. These deacons can administer many of the sacraments, and they can provide the liturgy with the linguistic and cultural flavor that the Hispanic communities demand. As for the Hispanics, the presence of deacons from their own numbers reinforces their commitment to participation in the church. Soon, however, the sheer numbers and the growing influence of the Hispanic deacons in their communities will prompt questioning.

The diaconate is no more or less permanent than any of the other sacred orders received by priests or bishops. The only sense in which current deacons are permanent is an exclusionary one: they are barred from progressing into the full priesthood. American bishops now accept that barrier as permanent. But nevertheless it may come up for serious debate if pastoral concerns, rather than arbitrary decisions on church discipline, become paramount in church policy. The issue might become a more urgent one should the division between deacons and full priests and bishops acquire an ethnic or racial tinge, with Hispanics alone confined to the lower orders of the ministry.

Meantime there is a surprising religious optimism among Hispanic priests, deacons, and religious men and women. They foresee a new day in which social action will be an integral concern of pastoral action. They see their ministry of attention to spiritual needs as one element of a wholly redemptive undertaking, of which social progress cannot be a separate or optional part. There is a profound theological understanding behind this new approach. This is producing a vitality that is one of the brightest lights on the horizon of the American church today.

Among the Hispanic bishops now leading the church in the U.S. are Mexican Americans, Puerto Ricans, other Latin Americans, and a Spaniard. They are diverse in personality—from the ebullience of Patricio Flores, Archbishop of San Antonio, to the solemn elegance of Roberto Sánchez, Archbishop of Santa Fe. However different their temperaments, there is a remarkable unity of purpose among them, which includes a sense of taking sides with the Hispanic people and of making the church responsive to their needs. This group of bishops is becoming known

47

to the Hispanic communities outside their dioceses and across the nation, as testified by the gruelling travel schedules of these pastors.

Everywhere he goes Mexican Americans greet Flores as "our bishop." Wherever a leadership group assembles to plan for the Hispanic church they will invite Sánchez. Bishop Peña, of El Paso, is recognized as a theological leader. Auxiliary Bishop Juan Arzube, of Los Angeles, is helping people forget the confrontation at St. Basil Church. They have not only the responsibilities of their particular dioceses, but also the responsibilities of national leadership, in which they have to answer to a diversity of American Catholics. At the same time they must make sure that Hispanics are given their proper place in the interests and priorities of the American church. Always teaching, they have at the same time to continue learning themselves, attending to ever-evolving doctrinal developments, and, after reflection, absorbing them into their ordained, authoritative teaching.

The sheer size of their task is overwhelming. They must be at the forefront of the impatient, bursting Hispanic church and bring that movement to the heart of the American church. Some critics, impatient young clergy, have decried their leadership as indecisive and ineffective. But to change the orientation of the Hispanic ministry and, more important, of the American church is a huge undertaking for so few. It is an occasion for the biblical prayer that the Lord send more shepherds to an ever-increasing flock.

There is a similarity between the roles of the bishops and those of Hispanic leaders in business, social action, and politics. A successful Hispanic business leader is besieged by civic demands on his or her time far beyond those that an Anglo person in business would receive. Hispanics in government are expected, first, to outperform their Anglo colleagues, and, second, to offer an overall Hispanic leadership to their agency over and above the requirements of their job description. Such extra demands seem to fall to the lot of any minority person making it ever so moderately in the majority world—not unlike the situation of the Hispanic bishops in a predominantly Anglo church.

The Hispanic priests, at their own level of responsibility, have also accepted their leadership role. In 1970, they organized PADRES (*Padres Asociados para Derechos Religiosos, Educativos, y Sociales*). This group grew out of the association of the priests with the efforts of César Chávez to organize farmworkers in California. Several Chicano priests joined that movement from the start and provided religious leadership to the organizers and strikers. In organizing PADRES, they broadened their scope so as to be of service to all Hispanic groups. Though their membership is still limited to Hispanics, their deliberations are open to all other priests who serve the Hispanic minority.

PADRES is now a national organization whose goals and interests include a deep political and social understanding. It has adopted the policy of "conscientization," explained by Paolo Freire in his *Pedagogy of the Oppessed*. PADRES wants not only to serve the faithful but also to join them in the process of gaining their own power, which is the basis of true liberation. It was the primary force in creating the new awareness that led to the appointment of more Hispanic bishops. Its action has led to the increase in Hispanic candidates for the priesthood and to a renewed zeal for service to the Hispanic faithful.

PADRES is now at a crossroads. Its original militancy bore fruit in the American church, but in the new mood pervading the church and country militancy is regarded with suspicion. Young though it is, the organization must now adjust its thought and purposes in keeping with new circumstances, while consolidating its gains. It is now planning to admit all priests who serve Hispanic communities. The current head of PADRES, Claretian Father Luis Olivares, feels the organization's effectiveness will be increased by cooperating with the Anglo priests who are working with the Hispanic minority.

In 1971, a group parallel to PADRES was formed, under the name *Hermanas* (sisters). From the beginning it included sisters from all Hispanic national groups as well as Anglo members; and their membership is also open to women other than religious. Their leadership is nationwide, with the three co-presidents residing in California, Texas, and New York.

Historically the situation of Hispanic nuns in the U.S. has differed drastically from that of Hispanic priests, and the nuns have been divided into two distinct ways of life.

The first group were engaged in menial occupations. Latin American orders of women religious were invited to send groups of Spanish-speaking nuns to serve in rectories, seminaries, and infirmaries. They became cooks, laundresses, and house-cleaners, and their work did not come under the legal or social constraints that would have applied to secular domestic help, whose hire would have been more expensive and complicated. These sister-maids often had little formal education, and they were not encouraged to acquire any; often they did not even get an opportunity to learn English. And they almost never had a chance to be of direct service to Hispanics and to the poor.

The other type of Hispanic nuns in America were young women living in America who were attracted to the religious life. They were not many, for lack of education was and is an obstacle. Most American orders of nuns are engaged in teaching, social service, or running hospitals, and fluency in English is a requisite for acceptance. In fact, a young woman who was accepted had to renounce, together with secular life, any ties with the culture and language of her Hispanic community. And once admitted, she would be assigned to a hospital, a suburban school, or some other form of ministry unrelated to her Hispanic background.

The number of Hispanic nuns in America, unlike that of priests, is not definitely known. Those associated with *Hermanas* have adopted a commitment to people, expressed in the statement that they are "an organization that wants to keep itself aware of the suffering of our Hispano people ... caught in what sociologists call 'the helpless cycle' ... a vicious circle which enwraps us in an inability to act for our own cause. ..."

Their team style of government comes not only from their national solidarity but also from one of the main purposes of their organization: to create team ministries fully incorporated in the barrio, conscious of the concerns and cultural demands of their own people. Like other organizations of minority women, they work to overcome more than one form of injustice. They have suffered discrimination not only as members of an ethno-racial minority, but also as women. *Hermanas* is also acutely aware of the unfinished business that faces all women in the Catholic Church, including the full acceptance of their personal ministry, which claims freedom from all constraints based on gender.

PADRES and *Hermanas* share with one another and with the whole Hispanic church a mission and destiny that goes beyond ethnic spirit and liturgical reform. It is leading them into a profound theological revolution that stands to change the course of the American Catholic Church. Hispanics may have accused the church of not being there, but they do not intend to let it stay away. They are involved in bringing the church into their own struggle for progress.

Just why and just how has it happened that the Catholic Church has not been there for the Hispanics in America? This cloudy question becomes somewhat illuminated when one contrasts what the church failed to accomplish for the Hispanics with what it did accomplish for the ethnic European immigrants who were likewise handicapped by the inability to speak English.

The chief and best-known means that the church in this country employed was the institution of the national parish. This was a departure from the kind of parish found in Europe. The national parish had no fixed boundaries. It served all the people of a given nationality in a general area. In the national parish, people from the same country were served by their own church, and their own language and traditions were the basis of their church life. In major cities and in many smaller industrial towns Polish, German, Lithuanian, Italian, Slovak, Slovenian, and other national churches were common up until the 1960s, especially in the Northeast and Middle West. These parishes generally had parochial schools, and sometimes high schools, too. The national language was often used as a medium of instruction, which is to say that education was bilingual. The pupils learned English as well.

The presence of national Catholic Churches turned the church into a major force in the socio-political development of most European immigrant groups. The church was at the center of the white ethnic neighborhood. It was a source of social cohesiveness and social advancement. As the ethnic parishioners became Americanized and moved to the suburbs, it seemed that the church, too, became Americanized and followed them there. Perhaps this Americanization was the culmination of the church's struggle for acceptance in the mainstream, which was symbolized by the election of John F. Kennedy in 1960.

If so, there was a price to be paid for it. For to its critics, as the church has become more American it has become less Catholic. As Americanization of the church was increasing here, a different understanding of the church's mission was developing in the rest of the world. It is true that Vatican II stressed that a fundamental mission of the church was the search for "enculturation." Evangelization, according to the Council's teaching, is not only to preach a set of doctrines to a people, but by doing so to modify the cultural tradition of the people, so that the gospel may be able to grow in their own cultural setting.

Americanization may stand in the way of evangelization. Some contemporary Hispanic theologians decry the American church's inability to focus on evangelization, and believe that that lack underlies the unsatisfactory relationship between the church and Hispanics today.

Some say that the gospel was indeed enculturated in the Hispanic tradition, so that the Catholic faith became one of its main elements. But the way in which this happened was different from the way it happened in other American national groups: with the Hispanics the enculturation never carried over into church structures. As a result, neither in colonial times nor afterward was there a truly native Hispanic clergy in sufficient numbers to nationalize or enculturate the church structures themselves. This may be a deeper explanation for the scarcity of Hispanic priests which was discussed earlier.

Except in the case of Hispanics, the American church has never been faced with a minority population of Catholics who were without their own native clergy. This may help to explain why the American church has had such difficulty incorporating itself in the Hispanic culture, and its inability to become a decisive force in the social progress of Hispanics.

Hispanics do not accept the marginal role they are now playing in the church. But as a minority of the poor, Hispanics in the church have called their destined role prophetic. A prominent Cuban American priest, Father Mario Vizcaíno, has described that prophetic role as a dual one: to *announce* the gospel, and to *denounce* the deviations from that gospel that are found in the structures of the establishment. Father Vizcaíno insists that both of these activities combined constitute the mission of Catholic Hispanics in the American church: they are to continue announcing the priority of the poor in that church—the heart of the gospel message—and being a spur in the side of the established church until it is remade into a community of believers and is not just a social or political organization.

4

American Catholics, Hispanic Variety

Most Hispanics would answer the question, "Are you a Catholic?" with a simple yes. They may add that they were baptized, they attended Catholic schools, they were married in the church, and so on. But the questioner should be aware that that for a Puerto Rican or a Mexican American being a Catholic has a different meaning than for an Irishman or a Pole.

For one thing, the answer from a Hispanic Catholic to the follow-up question, "Do you attend Sunday Mass?" might very well be no. This illustrates what might be the most striking difference between Hispanics and other American Catholics. The characteristic is not new; it existed long before the changes in the '60s that caused many American Catholics to stop attending religious activities on a regular basis.

For Hispanics, religion is a personal thing: the institutional church does not necessarily relate to their religious experience. Being a Catholic is a set of beliefs, rituals, relationships, and even behaviors. But it does not necessarily include full participation in an organized church, with structures, authority, and obligations.

There are many manifestations of this attitude. For instance, Hispanics are not likely to contribute as heavily or regularly to the support of the church as do non-Hispanics. A survey in the northeast United States asked Hispanics the question, "How much do you contribute to the church?" Only 17 percent answered "much"; the rest of the answers ranged from "little" to "almost nothing."

The amount of their contributions is of course influenced by the fact that Hispanics are relatively poor. But that would be only a partial answer. Much more important is the lack of feeling of belonging, of "owning" those church structures, and consequently of having a sense of responsibility to maintain them and to secure their financial subsistence. Practical details increase this alienation. The custom of using envelopes for making contributions seems to be outside the Hispanic cultural experience.

Hispanics can therefore be said to be religious, but at the same time "unchurched." In the past, most Catholics have associated their church with a sense of obligation. Rules of behavior and attendance were imposed by authorities. It might be that this very sense of obligation would prompt Hispanics to avoid regular attendance or participation. They might feel guilty about not attending Sunday Mass, and even confess it as a sin, but their defiance of the rules—even those supposedly imposed by God—can give a feeling of self-respect and self-worth. And perhaps underneath it all there is the intuitive understanding that these obligations do not come from God, but from human authorities, however legitimate.

The causes of this *despego*—this detachment—of Hispanics from church structures may be many. But it is clear that in America it separates them from other Catholics and is a reason for a lack of understanding between Hispanics and the American hierarchy.

Even though ordinary Hispanics may feel themselves distanced from church structures, their religiosity is nevertheless very real and permeates every aspect of their lives. It centers on two main areas: ritual and ethical codes.

Hispanic Catholicism is rich in ritual. The abstract theological dogma of the church is often too intellectual to arouse the interest of the common people. But there is a joyous, personal relationship between God and the Hispanic Christian. This God is not distant and forbidding, but is truly a father, the patriarch of a numerous and heavenly family. The Virgin Mary, the saints, the dead— one's own family—make for a lively, varied religious life. There is then a set of ritual celebrations that flesh out those relationships between the faithful and this large, happy family in heaven. There is the *fiesta* of the patron saint—in many cases the saint after whom the town was named. There are offerings, at times at great personal and financial sacrifice. There is a dialogue, even a sense of bargaining, in prayer. An exchange will be offered for a favor received: a candle will be lit, a pilgrimage will be made, the news of a favor granted will be published, and the promises will be faithfully kept.

At times an element of folk religion will be added to these relationships with the presence of the *curandero*, the visionary, the spiritual healer. The supernatural component of these practices varies, ranging from the simple *curandero*, who may be nothing more than a folk healer with an arcane knowledge of plants and other healing devices, to the complex structure that underlies the practice of the *santería*, with a hierarchy of spirits and a specific knowledge of their powers or special areas of concern. These practices all have in common a sense of ritual, formal and demanding, that is necessary to establish the desired relationships with the supernatural world. Some of these rituals are but "baptized" versions of ancient beliefs, predating Christianity in the Western Hemisphere, with influences from pre-Columbian or African cultures.

The sense of ritual that is characteristic of Hispanics emphasizes the personal, individual contact of each person with God and God's world. Many Hispanics consider only those sacraments relevant that mark milestones in a person's life: Baptism, Marriage, and the sacrament of the dying. To these, the sacrament of Penance may be added, in that it provides a cleansing sense to people beseiged by a basic feeling of inadequacy in their relationships to God. In the modern Hispanic church in America, the Eucharist has the potential of becoming important in the minds of the people insofar as it fosters a sense of community in celebration.

The religious practice of the Hispanic people, with its emphasis on a personal relationship with God and the saints and its disregard for the structured work of the church, has been described as vertical to distinguish it from the more "horizontal" involvement that characterizes the rest of the American church. The description has merit in that it points up a cause for the estrangement between Hispanic and non-Hispanic Catholics in this country. But it overlooks a more profound element of Hispanic religiosity—a horizontal dimension that finds its source in a collective sense of belonging that is at the heart of Hispanic moral behavior. This sense of collectivity is present among Hispanics in a degree unique to them, and may transcend the Spanish influence and be historically rooted in pre-Columbian influences.

This sense of community has been noted in studying the learning process of Hispanic children. Castañeda and other proponents of "cultural democracy" have found Hispanic children to be more "environment-affected," while their Anglo counterparts are more "environment-independent." The Mexican American child, for example, will put more effort into studying when that effort is made as part of a team. The Anglo pupil finds individual competition more of a spur to classroom effort.

The primary expression of this sense of collectivity is in the family. Even after many years in this country, the Hispanic retains a strong, multi-layered family structure, including not only the immediate parental family but also other relatives as part of an enlarged unit. Nor are these primary social links limited to blood relatives. Town of origin, for instance, provides a further tie to the institution of *compadrazgo* (literally translated as coparenthood) that connects neighbors as well as relatives. Quasi-familial relationships are also established on religious grounds: the role of the *padrino* (godparent) is taken very seriously by Hispanics who understand the life commitment that such sponsorship implies. *Padrinazgo* (godparenting) therefore extends beyond baptism into marriage sponsorship, and even to less crucial life changes, such as the celebration of the *quinceañera*—a girl's 15th birthday and her passage into womanhood.

These family and community structures carry with them a profound religious significance. Faithfulness to these extended collective relationships is an important part of the Hispanic sense of moral righteousness. The social and political movements engaged in by Hispanics in the '60s and '70s went to great lengths in attempting to identify the cultural characteristics that made Mexican Americans unique. The sense of closeness and collectiveness was labeled *carnalismo,* a word that cannot be translated. It implies relationships that come close to flesh-and-blood ties, and includes the sharing of the common interests, traditions, and moral commitments implied in such ties. The concept thus expressed in secular terms also has profound theological implications.

The two levels of understanding of the idea of horizontality we have been discussing, springing from differing cultural perspectives and ultimately with different depths of meaning, illustrate to some extent the substantial conflict existing between Hispanics and Anglos in the American church today. Hispanics seem to be saying there is a better, more purposeful sense of collectivity inherent in the Christian message, one that expresses itself in personal community relationships rather than the structured approach of an established hierarchical church.

Underlying these differences is a further element influencing the role to be played by Hispanics in the Catholic Church. Pope Paul VI, in his address to the Hispanic Second National Encounter, exhorted those in attendance not to put aside their popular religiosity. And in his encyclical *Evangelii Nuntiandi* he set the tone for a search by Hispanics for a place in the American church. The Pope said: "Christ carried out this proclamation [of his gospel] . . . by innumerable signs. . . . Among all those signs there is the one to which he attaches great importance: 'The humble and the poor are evangelized,' become his disciples, and gather together in his name the great community of those who believe in him. . . ."

In this context, the Hispanics, a poor and ethno-racial minority in the American church, represent a challenge reflecting the dilemma that has faced the church since

American Catholics, Hispanic Variety

Constantine made Christianity the official religion of the Roman Empire: Whether the primary allegiance of the established church as a human as well as a spiritual institution is to the poor or to the power structures of the social and political world.

The dilemma is present in the American church today, in spite of the fact that throughout its history the American political system has taken pains to separate church and state. The American church has accepted that separation to the extent that it refers to direct intervention in the current administration's policies or political party platforms. But it plays a major role as an institution, by virtue of its size and the type of acceptance that church leadership enjoys, in shaping public views and general political trends.

Hispanics are aware of that political force and the role the American church plays in the country. Faced with their own position of powerlessness, they have demanded that the church take a leading role in the struggle for equality they are engaged in. They have been disappointed. Various surveys have underlined this yearning and this disappointment: When asked whether the Catholic Church is sensitive to their needs, a majority of the respondents in a poll taken in the Northeast answered no. Similar feelings are expressed regarding the accessibility of priests by the people and whether the church has had any impact nationally in improving the economic conditions of Hispanics.

It would be inaccurate to say flatly that the Catholic Church has not assisted in the economic and social progress of Hispanics. Activities such as the leadership of the church in the question of undocumented aliens, the funding efforts of the Campaign for Human Development, and the services provided by the various diocesan-based Catholic Charities are all examples of assistance offered to the Hispanics by the church.

Perhaps the root of the disappointment is the fact that these church activities are peripheral and from the outside of the Hispanic communities. As the Hispanic communities have been described as unchurched, the American church could be called un-Hispanicized. Some Hispanic leaders have put it bluntly. In dealing with this minority, the American church has adopted as the first priority the *Americanization* over the *evangelization* of the Hispanic people.

It might be said that similar priorities have been present in the church's missionary activities throughout the centuries, when priests and religious men and women were the carriers not only of a spiritual message, but also of the cultural baggage accepted as "civilization" to the peoples they were to evangelize. The aftermath of World War II and the rush to decolonize the world have made the idea of importing a so-called civilization obsolete.

In the religious realm, the Second Vatican Council emphasized evangelization as the primary concern of the church, with a goal of cultural pluralism rather than domination by a single culture. Some Hispanics see their current efforts as a mission to get the American church to begin to understand the implications of the Vatican II teaching.

The conflict of evangelization versus Americanization needs to be resolved all the more urgently because the Hispanics are already Christians with a long religious tradition. As they become more aware of their identity and their position in the search for equality and justice, the distance between leaders and pastors may grow wider rather than narrower.

If the American church structure finds it difficult to accept Hispanics fully in its midst, it may point to the need for applying the theologically venerable concept of the collegial "sense of the faithful" as a guide for a rich and divinely inspired incarnation of the revealed truth in a church living in a secular world. In this sense, the Hispanics are offering the American church the opportunity to return to a tradition that they themselves refuse to give up. Hispanic religious leaders plan to build on specific traditions: the *Posadas* (lodgings), the folk-religious Christmas procession where Mary and Joseph are accompanied as they seek shelter and Jesus is about to be born; the *Semana Santa* (Holy Week), including the visits of condolence to the Blessed Mother on the death of her son; the painful meditation on the Last Words uttered by Jesus on the cross, and so on. These observances will continue to provide the Hispanic faithful with the deep life-and-death emotional involvement that is at the basis of the messianic revelation. Only after such painful experiences can the Christian fully rejoice in the Resurrection.

This type of faith experience involving the whole person may seem incompatible with the more intellectual practices of the Anglo faithful, which appear to the Hispanic too cold and cerebral. But there is no sound theological basis for valuing one above the other. It may be that the acceptance of cultural variations like this will prove to be the best contribution Hispanics have to offer the American church. When asked about Hispanics, the typical Catholic will respond in terms of a "problem" to be solved: poverty, lack of education, lack of native clergy, lack of participation in church activities. The Hispanics themselves consider their communities to be the best opportunity for the American church to rediscover its soul.

Finding joy and sorrow in the expression of faith, the ability to bring religious experience out in song and liturgy are recognized as a real contribution to the American church by the Hispanic community. But their leaders are concerned that it does not go deep enough; stopping at this level is akin to the condescending attitude of praising blacks for their sense of rhythm. These Hispanic leaders claim for their communities the role of reteaching the American church its historic sense of pluralism, with its wealth of cultural varieties and mutual acceptance that was a unique characteristic of the church in the United States. If these leaders are right, the "browning" of the American church may indeed be a revolution, as well as a return to its own best traditions.

These changes are still far off. It seems to some Hispanics that pluralistic acceptance is something only given to other Christian denominations. And as a result of this, some feel that in one or two more generations the intellectual leadership of the Hispanics, to the extent that it has any religious concern at all, will be in the hands of other than Catholics.

The dynamics of the relationship between Hispanics and the church in the United States are played against a background that both Anglos and Hispanics refer to, in different contexts: Latin America. For the American Catholic hierarchy, attention to Hispanics in this country is often a reflection of a need they first perceived in Latin America. The meetings of the Latin American Bishops Council

(CELAM) at Medellín and Puebla redirected the thought of the church in those countries. Despite the controversies that were engendered, church efforts in those countries were refocused by renewing or making new commitments to the poor and marginated in those societies. The movements were carefully observed by the American hierarchy.

The new directions of the Latin American church may not be fully understood in this country, but the American hierarchy, while being wary of socialistic elements, evidently recognized the power and vitality of the trend that the doctrinal developments were releasing in Latin America. On reflection, they were able to look upon Hispanics in the United States as their own domestic Latin America. In so doing, there was the danger that Hispanics would continue to be seen as a foreign group, in need of an old-fashioned missionary effort. But at least the effect was that more attention was paid to the Hispanics in the American church, even though the bishops are apparently not yet ready to move from evangelization and assistance programs to join in a mutual search for justice for this group.

Hispanic Catholic leaders approach their ties with Latin America in a more personal way. Conscious of the "suffering of our Hispano people," they see their struggles in the United States as similar to those in Latin America. As members of a minority they consider oppressed, they blame the economic woes of Latin America on the same financial and political forces at work in the oppression of minorities in the United States. With this feeling of unity, they accept the intellectual and ideological leadership from Latin America. From both Anglo and Hispanic viewpoints, then, Hispanics in this country have come to be considered a bridge between North and South America. Some Hispanic leaders object to the image, because "a bridge is meant to be stepped on," but they do see Hispanics in both hemispheres as partners in the same liberation struggle.

The possibilities open to the Hispanic community in the American church—cooperating in the liberation movements in Latin America, assisting in redirecting the U.S. church, promoting a renewed sense of community—all these present fascinating vistas for the future. It may be asked, however, to what extent the average Hispanic Catholic shares in these visions.

The question is difficult to answer. For one thing, as a people Hispanics have an ingrained attitude of accepting things as they are—an attitude, almost fatalistic, that is the result of a long tradition of discrimination and poverty. Furthermore the emphasis in church teaching on patience, docility, and respect for the established order, with the expectation of balancing rewards in afterlife, has had great impact on the average Hispanic—particularly those in the lower economic strata who have internalized this docility and have narrowed their hopes for economic and political progress. In fact, the image of the church for many is that of an institution dedicated to keeping the poor and minorities quiet so as not to disturb the status quo.

In addition, some Hispanics, particularly first-generation immigrants, do not consider the U.S. to be their permanent home. Given the closeness of "the old country" and the less than enthusiastic acceptance they find in America, it is easy to think of themselves as temporary residents with the intention of returning "home" when they have done sufficiently well economically. Even if they never actually do return, they tend to tolerate the discrimination and adverse conditions and to feel no compulsion to work to change those conditions.

For second-generation Hispanics the situation is different. They are keenly aware of the discrimination and lack of opportunities afforded them. Their difference in attitude and expectations accounts for the tensions existing between generations that is characteristic of the Hispanic community in the U.S. today.

The moment is critical. The new theological understanding of the involvement of the church in transforming the social order has taken hold of the leadership of the Hispanic church in America. Their cry now is as a *pueblo de Dios en marcha*—a people of God on the go. And while many of the less powerful sing those words in worship with more of a poetic than a practical meaning, their leaders have started to make them a program for immediate action.

The two National Encounters for Hispanic Catholics, in 1971 and 1977, were significant events in putting the new attitudes into practice. In the 1977 meeting, carried out with a great deal of emotional involvement, Hispanic Catholic leaders, both clerical and lay, defined for themselves and accepted a mission as agents of change, not limited to their own communities, but to the entire church. They recalled the role of the poor in the church and realized that their condition as an ethnic-racial minority differed from that of the blacks who were never in the Catholic Church in large numbers. But as poor and as a minority, Hispanics felt called upon to witness and to press to make a reality of the proclaimed church commitment to

67

the oppressed. Thus understood, their role becomes central to the Kingdom.

The Catholic hierarchy of the United States has started to take notice. At the May, 1980 bishops' meeting in Chicago, one afternoon of the two-day session was devoted to Hispanics and was followed by a Spanish liturgy in a Chicago barrio. The distance between the Hispanics leading the discussion and the participant bishops was evident, but the very existence of the dialogue gave rise to hope. Only time will tell if the dialogue will bear fruit. At stake, if it does, is a new American church.

5

Hispanics in the '80s:
A New American Leadership

In Washington there is an organization that lobbies with some success for Hispanic causes. Not as effective or well known as the established groups created by black leadership over the years (such as the Urban League or the NAACP), the National Council of La Raza does exert some pressure on legislators and can obtain for Hispanics the kind of visibility leading to substantial socio-economic gains.

Its director is Raúl Yzaguirre, a thoughtful, committed young man with clear vision. His answer to the question of what is the most urgent concern of Hispanic communities today is *empowerment*. With that word he identified the characteristic need of Hispanic groups and their program for action. Hispanics today are barred from the councils of power, as they are from education and other social and political arenas.

Yzaguirre was then asked what kind of program he would propose to attain that empowerment. His answer was simple but full of implications: "We must engage in *institution building*"—institutions that are Hispanic, that live for and are committed to the betterment of Hispanics, that can respond to their needs and aspirations, and even formulate their unspoken wishes.

For the director of the National Council of La Raza one such institution is the Catholic Church. It is there; it professes a commitment; it is powerful. As a member of that church and a deeply religious man, Yzaguirre's faith in the church includes a hope to change it, to restore it to the forefront in the struggle for liberation and progress for Hispanics in America.

Conversations with other Hispanic leaders in this country might lead to the conclusion that Rául Yzaguirre is in the minority. Many of these leaders find the church irrelevant in their social and political struggle.

Perhaps unlike other groups, Hispanics have not been particularly prone to creating specific political or social structures. Often, as is the case with other groups, the associations more likely to thrive are those geared to socializing, and held together by local origin, or by sporting or civic celebrations. However there has been a tradition of organizing. From the revolutionary concerns of Ricardo Flores Magón in the early days of the Mexican Revolution, to the *Mano Blanca* (white hand) which was a defense organization, there have been labor organizations and political groups throughout the history of Hispanics in the Southwest and East.

Most often, those organizations were topical responses to specific issues or concerns which faded away as the problem was either solved or seen to be insoluble. Perhaps the poverty of resources, both financial and psychological, was also a reason for the impermanence of these groups.

In reviewing some of the organizations active in this country today, it is well to remember their tendency to emphasize a particular aspect of their cause, regardless of the national origin of the group. For a long time two Puerto Rican groups were at odds because one, the *Boricuas*, put much stock in a nostalgic yearning for their home island. The other, calling themselves *Ricans*, defiantly emphasized their commitment to the continent, their consciousness of the hostile environment, and their will to succeed, both politically and culturally, in that environment. The differences between the two groups are much less important than their common interests.

The American G.I. Forum is the Hispanic organization for veterans. It was founded in 1948 by Dr. Héctor García. The occasion was the return of the body of Pvt. Félix Longoria, a World War II hero, to his native town of Three Rivers, Texas. He was denied burial in the local "for Anglos only" cemetery. Eventually, thanks to the intervention of then Congressman Lyndon B. Johnson, Longoria was buried with full military honors at Arlington National Cemetery.

Dr. Héctor García and those with him were disappointed at the indifference of mainstream veterans organizations to the plight of that Mexican American and started the Forum. Initially for Mexican American Veterans (with an Auxiliary for women), lately the organization has endeavored to recruit other Hispanics as well.

The Forum, born of that defense need, has always mingled its loyalty and war-time nostalgia with an interest in the social and political progress of Hispanics. The visitor to an American G.I. Forum convention may see very little difference from those of other veteran groups, the American Legion, Veterans of Foreign Wars, and so on. There are legionnaire caps, the pledge of allegiance and presentation of colors, patriotic speeches, and the rest. The Forum, like the other veteran organizations, has aged. The bulk of the Vietnam veterans have not joined.

Still, politicians and other leaders would ignore the

Forum at their peril. It is an established group, blue collar, loyal, and probably boasts among its members more registered voters than most other Hispanic organizations.

Members of the Forum can point with pride to the role of Hispanics in the defense of America at war. To those for whom patriotism matters most, Hispanics can point out that 37 Hispanics from 1863 to 1973 have received the Congressional Medal of Honor in the United States, the largest single ethnically identifiable group in the honor list.

The Forum builds on that pride and that debt. At a recent national convention, a young Chicano Navy Lieutenant listened respectfully as those heroes were memorialized. Then he whispered to his table-mate: "Medals of Honor are a good thing. It's a pity that most of them are granted posthumously. . . ." In his mind, and the purpose of the Forum, is the implication that Hispanics have been found worthy of dying for the country, but it is not clear if they will be accepted to live in it.

Military service has had another important impact on Hispanics, particularly Mexican Americans. Enlisted or drafted, there were substantial numbers of Hispanics in the Armed Forces, particularly in World War II and since. The G.I. Bill and other veterans' benefits were a major influence in integrating many Mexican Americans into the country's mainstream. The G.I. Bill specifically was responsible for a large increase in the number of Hispanics able to obtain college degrees. The Armed Forces have continued in this way to affect the development of educational and economic leadership for this group.

The American G.I. Forum often has cross-membership with the oldest major Mexican American organization in the country, the League of United Latin Citizens, LULAC.

LULAC was founded in the mid-20s as a defense organization, the result of difficult and farsighted negotiations among pre-existing Mexican American groups. Its aim was political action, focusing for the most part on citizenship, voter registration, and in some cases legal defense. With membership in most states where there is a large Mexican American population, LULAC in the last few years has invited other Hispanic groups to join, with little success. Today it remains a largely Mexican American organization. The leadership of these organizations can be described as middle-class, conservative, and nationalistic, often bound to ceremonies to the point where their critics have at times described them as social clubs.

These groups relate somehow to the Catholic Church: the American G.I. Forum, in true veteran fashion, has its own national chaplain and its local chapters around the country are expected to have one as well. LULAC invites the church hierarchy to all its major functions.

These two, the largest mass organizations among Hispanics, have in the recent past acquired a new role. Politicians, notably since the Nixon administration, have relied heavily on them to reach Mexican Americans and other Hispanics. An intelligent payoff was extracted by their leaders for this attention: the creation in the early '70s of SER—Jobs for Progress, a massive employment and training project for Hispanics, a result of major government grants to the American G.I. Forum and LULAC.

In the last couple of years, LULAC has been fortunate to have as its national president Rubén Bonilla, a young Texas lawyer. He has embarked during his tenure on a one-man national antidefamation, awareness-raising, political-demand campaign for Mexican Americans and all Hispanics, in speeches, rallies, and in meetings with leadership both inside and outside of the Hispanic world. He works zealously for the unity and political coalition of Hispanics at the national level for common purposes.

Bonilla could be considered a prototype of the new Hispanic political leadership in the '80s. His view of the Catholic Church in Hispanic affairs is one of dismay. Although he himself is a religious person, he sees the established church in America as alien, irrelevant to the urgent political and social agenda of the Hispanics. He is aware of the isolated efforts of the Hispanic Secretariat at the National Conference of Catholic Bishops (NCCB), and cooperates with it in common efforts. But he sees the organized church as unmoved by those efforts and essentially hostile to, or at best unconcerned with Hispanic problems.

The office of Secretariat for Hispanic Affairs of the NCCB represents a major hope for the future. It is very hard to describe, possibly because the goals assigned to it by the hierarchy may not be consonant with the impact the Secretariat is having in the Hispanic church, and in the Hispanic secular world as well. The prime force behind the Secretariat is the director, Pablo Sedillo, a layman with a vision and a dedication that have carved for him a special place in Hispanic leadership today. Firmly grounded in theology, and aware of its implications for social justice, the Secretariat has become the presence of the organized church among communities of belief throughout the Hispanic world. Charged with a pastoral mission, the Secretariat has regional centers, with a relationship to the local religious authorities that varies in each region. But Sedillo has understood pastoral care in the context of social action, and both at the national level and in the regions, he has immersed the individuals connected with his work in the middle of political and social action.

The Secretariat has been responsible for calling the two major conventions of Hispanic Catholics, the National Encounters, and for bringing Hispanic interests into the mainstream of the American church at the Call to Action meeting in Detroit in 1976. It has also fostered increased understanding of Hispanics by the American hierarchy and supported the development of Hispanic theological and social thought—for instance, through the work of the Mexican American Catholic Cultural Center in San Antonio, Texas.

At the other end of the political spectrum, away from the veterans' loyalty of the Forum, the mainstream political action of LULAC, and pastoral-social action of the Hispanic Secretariat, Hispanics have also over the years formed other groups with a more militant profile. The '60s and early '70s saw an explosion of radical political organizations. They were the Hispanic version of the new minority awareness, exemplified in the "Black Is Beautiful" slogan, and in the Black Panthers, SNCC, and so on.

The Hispanic version was the result of reflecting, taking stock, and returning to old values that could create a sense of peoplehood. The leaders of these groups revived the old symbolic name of Aztlán, the mythical "land of the North," and they saw themselves as the true descendants of Aztlán and its primitive, original people.

The question of identity is quite important when a minority attempts to define itself. In this case, Mexican Americans, for instance, wanted to find a place between America and Mexico. More important, they had to find a cultural identity, defiantly their own, in a society that defined them as *nonwhites,* out of the mainstream, a minority. A Puerto Rican scholar has defined the central role of culture in that context: "Culture awareness," said Seda Bonilla, "is the minority's defense against internalization of the stigma" attached to that minority by the surrounding community.

MAYO (the Mexican American Youth Organization), La Raza Unida, MAPA (Mexican American Political Association), MECHA (Chicano Student Movement of Aztlán) were organizations created under this new sense of cultural defense.

They all were heavily intellectual groups, and they flourished on college campuses. All their leaders were aggressively anti-church. They saw the church as another manifestation of the oppressive system they were fighting. There was in their ideology an empathy for religious practices as practiced by the common people, but finally they rejected even those as manifestations of a spurious component of their cultural identity, relics of the Spanish intervention on the continent, which they also rejected as they stressed their native origins.

Among the Puerto Ricans, about the same time, the revolutionary spirit was best exemplified by the Young Lords Party. This group started as a youth gang in Chicago's Lincoln Park area. They evolved into an organization concerned with the local politics of displacement, as poor Puerto Rican families were moved from that area westwards to make room for urban renewal, luxury high-rises. The Lords then developed into a highly ideological political movement, immersed in the purest Marxist-Maoist orthodoxy. The Party was unusual in that it was exported from Chicago to New York, and its beginnings there were hailed as the start of a new consciousness for Puerto Rican people and heightened hopes for effective liberation. Alfredo López, in his *Puerto Rican Papers,* has described that hope and that beginning.

These radical organizations have lost membership or even disappeared as the committed and cause-prone '60s gave way to the more conservative, mainstream late '70s. In their wake, they left the sense of pride and people-identity they stressed, as well as the raised consciousness that generates continued action. There also remains the viewpoint that the church is just one more establishment institution and a feeling of doubt that such a church will ever be relevant to the unfinished Hispanic agenda.

There are other organizations as well among Hispanics. In the short span of ten years, IMAGE, an association of Hispanic government employees at the federal, state, and municipal levels, has become one of the most influential Hispanic groups in the country. Started as a Mexican American group, IMAGE has managed to expand its membership to all Hispanic national groups. At a recent election of officers, their leadership included Mexican Americans, Puerto Ricans, and even a Spaniard.

Today, IMAGE is one of the three major Hispanic organizations, along with LULAC and the American G.I. Forum. The growth of such a young association was easy to foretell. As government employees, its white-collar members are more educated than the average Hispanic. They know about political and government processes, and are able to use government resources and policies, such as affirmative action programs, to their advantage.

IMAGE, however, is more than a professional-advancement organization for its members. It attempts to influence the political and administrative processes to benefit the Hispanic communities at large. IMAGE is an establishment group, but it is not concerned with the trappings and rituals of older organizations, instead concentrating on action towards political goals. Among the rituals they have discarded is any type of church role in their organization. When asked, IMAGE leaders simply point to the irrelevance of that church structure for the tasks they have set for themselves.

This type of action-oriented organization has several counterparts, concerned primarily with change through service. ASPIRA (aspire, yearn for) is a Puerto Rican educational agency, founded by Antonia Pantoja in the '60s to aid the aspirations of young Puerto Ricans for a college education. But it does more than provide counselors to guide the youth through the preparation and application process. It also promotes school clubs where the youths train in leadership and devote time to learn more about their cultural background and thus achieve a sense of group identity.

LULAC has developed a similar service, the LULAC Educational Services, concentrating on encouraging college aspirations in Mexican American youths.

This emphasis on college education shows that the Hispanic leadership has learned the lesson from the progress made by American blacks. It was a new generation of college-educated black professionals that brought about the substantive changes in American society from the time of *Brown vs. Board of Education* in 1954. At that time, the full measure of the impact of the Negro colleges started to be felt.

Hispanics today do not have a system of colleges parallel

to that of blacks. There is no major university in the United States run by and for Hispanics. The only means for building leadership is through entrance into mainstream institutions of higher education, where individuals can be trained in competition and at the same time acquire a sense of responsibility as future leaders in their communities.

Other organizations in Hispanic communities are also single-purpose. Among them are the Mexican American Legal Defense and Education Fund (MALDEF) and the Puerto Rican Legal Defense and Education Fund (PRLDEF). Their task, initially funded heavily by major foundations, is to carry the struggle for justice for Hispanics to the courts. Their success has been great, particularly considering their size and resources. Not only have they brought litigation for bilingual education, the right of the Hispanic child not to be sent to a class for the mentally retarded on the basis of an English test, the ending of segregated schools and other facilities, full human rights for immigrants, and so on, they have also constituted a primary advisory network on the impact and the eventual meaning of progressive legislation planned or enacted.

In observing a few of the organizations and leadership activities of Hispanics in this country, a pattern seems to emerge: structurally there are great differences in cohesiveness. Many groups were organized in response to a single issue. In the more stable organizations, the more successful and action-oriented groups, there seems to be a strong sense of secularization and a lack of any church contact. This alienation is greater in the younger organizations and in those that have a more professionally trained leadership.

An unexpected characteristic of the state of organizing among Hispanic communities is the pattern of collective leadership. In a cultural tradition that historically has singled out individuals for leadership and personal allegiance (Francisco Villa in Mexico, Pedro Albizu in Puerto Rico, Martí in Cuba, for instance), Hispanics in the United States have not had a charismatic leader like Martin Luther King, Jr. Individual leadership, while effective and farsighted, has not been able as a rule to capture the imagination of the Hispanics as a group, or of non-Hispanics around them.

A major exception to this generalization is the charismatic figure of César Chávez, the leader of the California farmworker movement. The national press, several books, radio, and TV have narrated the story of that movement. The grape-harvesting workers' plight and later on that of the lettuce pickers are probably the two Hispanic issues that have affected Americans at large the most. The boycott of grapes or lettuce reached into the homes of many progressive Catholics and others concerned with social-justice issues for as long as it took for Chávez to achieve victory.

Religion, and eventually the church, was very much present in the farmworker struggle. It was no accident. As a grass-roots organizer, and because of his own deeply felt personal beliefs, Chávez made religion central to his organizing strategy.

The farmworkers' movement had economic gains for its members as its ultimate goal. But to achieve that goal a process of consciousness raising was required that included the stressing of cultural identity in a dynamic, creative way, expressed in actions and symbols.

A New American Leadership

The farmworkers' eagle—with an Aztec flavor—was designed so that it could be easily reproduced even by those without particular artistic skills. The other most prominent symbol of that struggle was the banner of Our Lady of Guadalupe. These two symbols made their way into American households through TV reporting. Chávez's tactics had a religious aspect, with prayerful fasting as an expression of his commitment to nonviolence. The presence of the Virgin of Guadalupe in his rallies appealed to the sense of religious righteousness of the farmworkers. His marches, accompanied by the banner and rallying around a celebration of the Mass and reception of the Eucharist, took on the character of religious pilgrimages. Chávez, perhaps alone among Hispanic leaders in the United States, made his campaign a religious as well as a social-justice experience.

As a part of this strategy, Chávez attempted to enlist the forces of the organized church. His was a conscious effort to bring the established church—not only religion—to his and the farmworkers' side. Success in that second strategic aspect was mixed. Some of his collaborators have decried the slowness of the Catholic Church to accept the invitation to join the strikers. Some go so far as to say that real support for the "campesinos," the farmworkers, was never forthcoming from the church.

The church was indeed late in coming into the struggle, and horror stories circulated of church organizations, hospitals, and schools buying up grapes and lettuce at close-out prices as they ignored the boycott. But eventually it was the church leaders who became the only mediators acceptable to both parties in the dispute and the prime forces in securing the contract negotiations and agreements that marked victory for the farmworkers in the grape and lettuce fields.

The role of the church in the farmworkers' struggle might have been the single most concerned and influential act of assistance provided to Hispanics by the church in modern America. But the church perhaps benefited even more than the farmworkers from that action, at a different, more deeply theological, level. From the beginning of the farmworker struggle, even before the hierarchy took notice and acted, there was a group of priests with Chávez and his campesinos, independent of their bishops' will or even knowledge. Their commitment was similar to that of college-educated and other professional youths who felt a call and came to serve the farmworkers and César Chávez, their leader. For the priests and religious people, this campaign represented their first coming together, as Hispanics or Hispanic sympathizers, with the purpose of serving a group of visible Hispanics, militantly seeking social justice. They benefited as much in gaining awareness of themselves as they provided ministering. Out of this experience would come a new commitment to Hispanics in the context of social action. Structurally, this priestly movement resulted in the first organization of Hispanic priests, PADRES, which since its creation has been a primary impetus for Hispanic church awareness.

The glory days of farmworker organizing have given way to the dreary continuing task of labor elections, contract negotiations, and slow gains for these workers. Defeats and successes have alternately characterized this struggle.

The fate of the migrant farmworker has not yet been

resolved. California is only one area where Hispanics (and blacks, Filipinos, and others) work in the fields. There are several farmworker migrant streams today: In the East, harvesting crops leads the workers northward, from Florida all along the Eastern Seaboard, all the way to Maine. From Texas and the Valley, a strong migratory current takes families North, to the Midwest, Ohio, Illinois, Wisconsin, and Minnesota, while other streams lead harvesting crews Northwest, all the way to Washington state.

The plight of those workers, mostly since the Chávez struggle, has made them known to social progressive forces and to the various relief and social services agencies, to the point that, although they are a minority of the total Hispanic population, Hispanics have come to be identified with migrant farmworkers in the public consciousness. Their living conditions are poor: leaving their home bases from late April until October, they follow the ripening crops, picking them at wages below the accepted minimums, and enlisting the entire family, including children, for the all-day work necessary to make the entire trek worthwhile. Their housing is provided by the grower, and its quality is such that, for instance, when the Colorado Advisory Committee to the U. S. Commission on Civil Rights attempted to examine those living conditions, it felt that visuals could tell the story better, and it produced a unique photographic report.

Children are taken from the schools before the school year ends. For a long summer they will trek from school to school, to special education programs in those school districts that establish them with federal funds, and they will be alternatively over-immunized or deprived of the necessary health care until they abandon schooling, many not having finished grammar school, to join their parents in the fields.

Farmworkers were found to have a life expectancy of 43 years, scarcely more than half that of Americans as a whole. Apart from childhood diseases and the hard working conditions, their health is threatened by exposure to the chemicals that are so integral a part of modern agriculture in the United States.

The numbers of these families are difficult to pin down. The federal government has since the '60s adopted a series of legislative measures, attempting to remedy some of the more striking abuses of the farmworker life: crew leader registration, a minimum time between application of chemical herbicides and workers' entering the fields, minimum housing conditions, and establishment of health clinics.

Only farmworkers who take advantage of government employment services come under the protection of these legislative actions. Many more arrange for their work independently, directly with the grower, and their work and living conditions remain unpoliced. This dual access to that type of work also makes it impossible to put a number on the size of this population. In the six Central States, for instance—Illinois, Indiana, Michigan, Minnesota, Ohio, and Wisconsin—Labor Department officials estimated the size of the migratory streams at 100,000 every year.

To many, the federal programs created to protect and assist the farmworkers are a form of price support for the growers. They argue that those services would not be necessary if wages and other working conditions reflected the real value of the job undertaken by those workers.

Significant improvement on those wage levels would have considerable impact on the prices Americans pay to set their tables.

César Chávez and his farmworkers constitute the most explicit instance of a "confessional" socio-political movement in the United States among Hispanics. Their leader's charisma is also unique. Other figures have captured the imagination of Hispanics in a personal way: Reies Tejerina in New Mexico and Texas led a group of followers for a while with a claim for historical justice on the issue of the land grants. His *Alianza Popular de los Pueblos Libres* (Popular Alliance of Free Peoples) focused on the aftermath of the Treaty of Guadalupe Hidalgo and the loss of lands of the inhabitants of the old Mexican territories.

In a different context, Rodolfo "Corky" González led Chicanos in Denver in a *Crusade for Justice* to face the power structures and improve their living conditions. His was not purely an economic goal but emphasized the sense of peoplehood of Chicanos, as the basis for a political and social movement.

Corky is the author of the major epic poem to come out of the Chicano experience: "*Yo soy Joaquín*," I am Joaquin; it begins:

> I am Joaquin,
> lost in a world of confusion,
> caught in the whirl of a
>   gringo society,
> confused by the rules,
> scorned by manipulation,
> and destroyed by modern society.

> My fathers
>   have lost the economic battle
> and won
>   the struggle of cultural survival.
>
> And now!
>   I must choose
>   between
>   the paradox of
> victory of the spirit,
> despite physical hunger,
>   or
>   to exist in the grasp
> of American Social neurosis,
> sterilization of the soul
>   and a full stomach....

After recalling a history full of struggle and defiance, Corky concludes: I SHALL ENDURE! I WILL ENDURE!

These Hispanic leaders vary in their relationships with the church, but they share a common sense of ideology, as in differing ways they agree in calling for a "primacy of the spirit."

A similar commitment is present in other Hispanic leaders, like Congressman Robert García. His office is in a walk-up in a public housing project in the Bronx, the largely Puerto Rican district he represents in Congress. Across the street is the imposing roman-column monument that houses the municipal courts. The son of a Protestant minister, Congressman García brings to his political life elements of that same ministry. He is intensely aware that his community needs many things, but he says that even if he could provide for them better housing, education, and income, that would not be enough. His constituency asks for more. "They need spirit," he says, the hope and the ability to look beyond the immediate, material wants to a sense of spiritual purpose, the only avenue to self-worth and direction. He would like, for instance, for the church to build public housing, even with federal funds, because, he feels, "the church alone could create homes and communities, rather than just housing units in a tract."

We have observed that one cannot fully judge the religious commitment of Hispanics by comparing their public observances and church allegiance with other national groups. The same is true in the area of social action.

The explicit religious element in the César Chávez symbols or the kind of direct church involvement proposed by Congressman García may not be typical of the attitude of Hispanic leaders. But even without these explicit manifestations, there is a deep religious component in the style and drive of many of them. Martin Marty has called the process a "secular ministry." Hispanic leaders are often moved by a sense of dedication that has religious characteristics. Their commitment becomes a sort of secular holiness that makes compassion and service to others the basis of their social and political activity.

This driving force may not be recognized as religious by the leaders themselves. A national proponent for bilingual education was asked what motivated her to continue the struggle. She simply pointed to the need of the Hispanic children to have a proper, equal education. When pressed, she indicated that she had been raised and educated in the

Catholic faith, but did not practice now and did not go to church. But the children are in need, and "somebody has to serve them. . . ."

The intensity of dedication to the tasks of social justice shown by these leaders can perhaps be best understood as a secular redirection of a deep religious commitment. Actual church-going does not seem related to the urgency of the tasks. Still, religious observances are often continued. The same educational leader related that when her efforts reached a political or administrative impasse and pressures mounted, she might on occasion send money to her mother in Puerto Rico to buy a candle and offer it to her favorite image of the Virgin Mary. . . .

Hispanic leadership and organizations show a variety of purposes and levels of effectiveness. Their history speaks of a response to issues and a continuing clarification of purpose. Looking at this history, the impression persists that the church has been and remains at the margin of these organizing efforts and leadership developments. Church relationships have not yet been completely discarded, but the trend is definitely in that direction.

The fact that the lack of adequate church involvement is still resented and regretted may indicate an opportunity the church might turn to its advantage, and so too is the zeal shown by Hispanic leaders that is akin to religious fervor. But without some change, the trend to complete secularization will evidently continue. This can better be perceived as one looks at the political and social issues central to the concern of Hispanic leaders today.

6

Who's Picking Up the Slack?

In 1978, the Gallup organization conducted a study of the attitudes of Hispanic Catholics toward their church for the Spanish-language newspaper *El Visitante Dominical.* When the question was asked, "Have you ever been approached by such groups as Evangelicals, Pentecostals, or Jehovah's Witnesses to convert to their religion or faith?" the response was considered by the pollsters to be "astonishing." Almost three-quarters of all Hispanic Catholics answered yes.

Proselytizing by Protestant groups seems especially prevalent among Hispanics in this country today—as it is also in Latin America. This impression can be reinforced by observing any large gathering of Hispanics in any city. Frequently, religious leaflets will be passed out urging people to convert into an Evangelical, Pentecostal, or similar religious group. The tone of the literature is quite direct and antagonistic: the tenets of the Catholic faith are wrong in their interpretation of the Scriptures; the Catholic clergy misleads the faithful; the only way to salvation is to accept the Christian message from this particular sect. The harshness of this propaganda is quite foreign to the current atmosphere of coexistence and friendly relationships among the religious denominations in this country.

The traditional commitment of Hispanics to the Catholic Church is not universally true today. Some have estimated the number of Hispanics belonging to Christian groups other than Catholic at 15 percent, but exact figures are not available. In their absence, a series of impressions strike the observer:

• In Los Angeles, the old Plaza, the original settlement of the *pueblo,* is central to the city's celebration of its 200th anniversary. Olvera Street, leading to the Plaza, has been refurbished and a Mexican market attracts tourists. On one side of the Plaza is the large Catholic church; across the Plaza on the corner of Olvera Street is the Methodist Spanish church.

• In Chicago, the Spanish Episcopal Services, a program of the Episcopal diocese, operates the first bilingual community college for Hispanics in the Midwest. An old movie studio in the Uptown neighborhood has been converted into the college building. It features a chapel as well, and what might be the only image of Our Lady of Guadalupe to be found in an Episcopal church!

• In the New York area there are an estimated 400 chapels and churches of Protestant denominations serving Hispanic congregations.

• The Mexican Baptist Bible Institute in San Antonio, Texas has 100 minister candidates. The nearby Catholic Oblate College Seminary has only 30 Hispanic seminarians.

• The Southern Baptist Convention, based in Atlanta, numbers 1500 Hispanic churches in America and is opening at least 150 more each year.

Why this increasing shift from the Catholic Church to the various Protestant churches? It is true that the post-Vatican II climate does not put such rigorous barriers between the Catholic Church and other Christian denominations. But the abandonment by many Hispanics of the church in which they were baptized and raised bears examination. It can tell much about this minority and the real or potential role of the church among them.

The increased allegiance of Hispanics to Protestant sects seems to be based on their desire for faith and service. It may be the current manifestation of the personal relationship to God that is characteristic of the Hispanic people. The case of a Cuban Calvinist minister is illustrative. A lawyer and political science professor at Havana University before the revolution, he had close relatives in the Catholic hierarchy in Cuba. After the Castro takeover, he left Cuba and engaged in lecturing and teaching at various universities in the United States and Latin America. One day, as he describes it, "God called me. He wanted me to work for him." He saw no room for a ministry in the Catholic Church—he was in his late 40s—so he entered a Calvinist college and in a couple of years was ordained a minister. Today he serves a large congregation of Hispanics in a major Midwestern city.

Similar incidents are occurring throughout the Hispanic communities. There is a thirst for faith there, and a vacuum which the Catholic Church seemingly cannot fill. Leaders of the Protestant churches maintain they are just "picking up the slack." A recent drive by Methodist leaders in the suburbs of Los Angeles to attract and enroll Hispanics was apparently done with the encouragement of local priests who were themselves unable to reach them.

However, the trend among Hispanics is less toward the "mainline" Protestant churches and more toward the Evangelical, the Pentecostal, and similar denominations. The emphasis in these groups is generally on emotional involvement in worship and in definite social activities, rather than on theological content. Observing Puerto Rican Pentecostal churches in Milwaukee, Samuel Betances found that the local congregation becomes the focal point for a family's social life. Members are required to attend at least two church functions every week. They are expected to follow strict rules of behavior, including dressing, eating, and drinking patterns, manner of speech, and so on, involving most aspects of the individual's life. And they stress solidarity in their community. As one former Catholic put it, "If I didn't show up at my old parish, nobody bothered to check out why."

Very few of these congregations own large, elaborate church buildings: storefronts are more the norm, very much in the pattern of the black congregations in the inner city.

As with the blacks, the deep commitment of Hispanics to these informal churches is the result of a mutual sense of belonging. The storefront church belongs physically to the specific congregation or its pastor; the individuals belong to the church because that is the one place where there are no authority pressures of class, and instead there is a sense of equality and self-worth not to be found in other social contexts of the city. As with the blacks, the religious outpourings in the small congregation become a natural release for those oppressed by poverty and discrimination because of racial or ethnic origin. The church in a sense provides the only place of liberation.

This liberating experience occurs mostly with less traditional church sects. It can take place because there is a class identification between pastor and congregation. Perhaps this characteristic is the most striking difference between these churches and the Catholic Church.

The Catholic priesthood is the culmination of a long, involved process that includes theological learning but also indoctrination in a middle-class, educated atmosphere. By contrast, becoming a minister in one of the more popular Christian denominations is a relatively simple process that is accomplished as much through part-time formal training as by means of apprenticeship with established ministers.

The result is that there is no dearth of indigenous Hispanic leadership among Spiritualists, Evangelicals, Pentecostals, and similar groups. Those churches create ministers as they need them, drawing them from the communities themselves. This leadership is thus identified and recognized, and, as it acquires prestige, will not limit itself to church activities but will cut across all aspects of the social life of the congregation.

So it is common to find Protestant Hispanic ministers at the forefront of their communities as they struggle for political representation, educational reform, community services, and all other forms of progress in social justice. This secular role is an extension of the minister's leadership. For the congregation, it is a natural development from the cohesiveness achieved through the church into action for political and social issues. How well this has worked in the past can be seen in the continuing role of black ministers in the justice issues of the secular world.

The ability of the Catholic priest to enter the political arena, on the other hand, is shaped by the type of total dedication to worship and ministry that is the natural extension of his long indoctrination. A bishop, when asked about the role of priests in the social and political fields, pointed to the "danger" that such activity would divert the priest from his mission, and eventually force him to leave the priesthood for a full-time dedication to secular action.

One may want to ask why the two areas must be so sharply separated in the Christian minister and whether the strict delineation of role is called for by the basic gospel message or by the historical interpretation of church discipline. Certainly there is a biblical demand for dedication to pastoral service, but in the same context there is also a call for action to serve the urgent "secular" needs of the poor.

The Catholic Church in America in the past found an indirect but effective way to assist previous immigrant groups in their search for social progress. Will it find it possible to do the same now for Hispanic groups?

Once more the discussion of Hispanics in the church leads to a reconsideration of the very mission of that church, as it defines itself in relationship to the poor. Some indications of hope for the future of that definition are to be found in movements such as the Community Organized for Public Service (COPS), the United Neighborhood Organizations (UNO), the Secretariat for Hispanics, and others. The question remains whether these attempts are isolated, or are the forerunners of a major revolution the American church has decided to embark on.

In the meantime many Hispanics are finding a more consonant response in other interpretations of the gospel message outside the Catholic Church. This development has some unsatisfactory effects. In the first place, at times there follows a sort of disenchantment that makes these Hispanics return to the Catholic Church to seek their religious expression there. These returnees will have considered their other religious practices insufficient, or have felt all along that only Catholicism provided the depth of religious experience they yearned for.

Of more concern is the potential for all those unstructured churches, lacking solid theological understanding, to stray into cults that are dangerous to the individual and to society. Those dangers are many: from the unscrupulous using of church structures as a front for economic profit, to the refusal of sect members to accept medical practices necessary on occasion to save lives, to the type of fanaticism that led so many black believers to the massacre of Jonestown.

The need for socio-political leadership may make many ignore those and similar dangers. There is a leadership now in Hispanic communities that is moving forward for social progress, that identifies itself as Christian but does not consider Catholicism to be the only avenue for that progress. Most of their success lies in the fact that they have stepped into the vacuum left in the social realm by the inaction of the Catholic Church.

7

The Political Future:
Hambre y Sed de Justicia

The future of Hispanics, as that of other groups, will take shape in the area of political action. For Hispanics, the driving force is *"hambre y sed de justicia"*—hunger and thirst for justice.

A recent study of the political attitudes, ideologies, and programs of the various Hispanic groups showed certain common interests among them, as well as some differences. The first common trait to emerge is their almost total lack of political participation and representation in American society. There are 100 senators and 435 representatives in Congress. Among those there is no Hispanic senator (after the defeat of Senator Joseph Montoya of New Mexico in 1974). There are five representatives, one of whom is the nonvoting commissioner from Puerto Rico. Significantly the Hispanic Congressional Caucus includes among its associate membership nearly 100 representatives and senators, almost all of whom have a significant number of Hispanics among their constituencies.

At the state level there are 7,562 legislators, of whom 80 have Spanish surnames. No state except New Mexico has Hispanic legislators in numbers proportionate to their Hispanic populations. Of the 302 other officials elected to state-wide office in the country only four are Hispanic, and all are in New Mexico. That state is also the only one where one can find Hispanics on the state Supreme Court.

Hispanics are also absent from elective office in major city governments. The Puerto Rican mayor of Miami is the only Hispanic among mayors in large American cities. Municipalities such as Los Angeles, with about one million Mexican Americans in its population, or Chicago, with a half million Hispanics of all national groups, have no Hispanics in their elected city councils.

This lack of representation is explained at times by a lack of involvement of Hispanics in the political process. As a group, they are perhaps the least likely to be registered to vote, or to vote even when registered. But the lack of participation itself needs to be explained. Vague cultural explanations are not sufficient. One must question further, and in doing so the socio-economic status of this minority becomes crucial to an answer.

It has been suggested that a minimum threshold of "economic leisure" must be reached before full participation in political life by a group or an individual can take place. Minorities—in America, racial minorities—that are too concerned with everyday economic survival do not have time for the less immediate concerns of political participation. Psychologists speak of a scale of needs and values where self-improvement—what they call self-actualization—comes only after the most urgent survival needs have been satisfied.

In that context, Hispanics are seen as a group to be concerned with survival issues, since indicators of social equality place them well behind the white majorities in the country. Hispanics on the average have an income only 50 percent that of the white majority, are likely to have completed a college education 25 percent as often as whites, and have an incidence of poverty that is three times as high as the white population. As a consequence, the concerns of Hispanics are often confined to social and economic needs: housing, education, employment, and so on. In that, they have much in common with other racial minority groups in the country. However, like other groups, Hispanics identify at times with specific foreign issues as well. And, finally, there are issues that combine both domestic and foreign political concerns.

In foreign policy, Hispanics as a group were favorable to the Panama Canal treaty negotiated by the Carter administration. Similarly, Hispanics favor a policy of friendship in other aspects of American relations with Latin America. A feeling of language and cultural affinity underlies this posture.

Chicanos have taken up the issue of immigration policy that spans both domestic and foreign policy concerns. They have made their concern the status of the so-called "illegal aliens." The Carter administration proposed early in 1977 a package of immigration laws that has been largely ignored by Congress. Mexican Americans and other Hispanics opposed the package. A Select Commission on Immigration and Refugee Policy was appointed, with instructions to report to the President and Congress in early 1981.

The history of immigration policies of the United States is full of contradictions between accepted ideological tenets—"a nation of immigrants," the welcome sight of the Statue of Liberty—and progressively restrictive policies. Present immigration laws are at times contradictory and enforcement selective, but they are always complex and confusing.

American immigration policies have affected Hispanics

in a very special way. From the beginning of the legislation restricting immigration (the Chinese Exclusion Law of 1882), race and ethnicity have been major factors. The Dillingham Commission appointed by Congress in 1907 completed its work in 1911 and in its 11 volumes of reports set the basis for the immigration policies of the United States that would remain in effect with minor changes until 1965.

Those policies, for the first time written into federal law in 1917, had as their explicit purpose the preservation of the "purity" of the national ethnic and racial stock present in America at the beginning of the century and the prevention of immigration of nonwhites and Southern European peoples. This preservation was to be accomplished by an elaborate system of national quotas for immigration from the various countries and the total prohibition of immigration from Asia and Africa.

This quota system did not apply to immigration from countries in the Western Hemisphere until 1965, when a more general system of immigration ceilings by hemisphere and individual country replaced the old quotas. But prior to 1965 there was some openness to immigration from Mexico, limited only by the availability of jobs and the mechanics of securing the appropriate documentation. When at various times in the '20s there were moves in Congress to restrict Mexican immigration, they were neutralized by the major employers of inexpensive Mexican labor, the railroads and agribusiness.

Immigration from Mexico was also the object of special policy features: the institutionalization of the "temporary workers," entering the country for specific times and work assignments in agriculture. This approach, called the bracero (farmhand) program, remained in existence in two phases from 1942 to 1964. The concept was utilized several years later by European countries in the so-called "guest worker" programs. In the United States, the bracero was not only limited in the length of stay but also restricted to a specific employer. The employer thus could control not only wages and working conditions, but also could determine the very presence of the worker in this country. Critics of this program have likened it to the indentured servitude of the early days of American settlement.

Apart from its impact on wages and working conditions, the bracero program also made labor organizing among farmworkers almost impossible. Only when unions and other liberal forces achieved the repeal of that program was the movement of César Chávez possible in California.

Repeal of the bracero program and the extension of immigration ceilings to immigration from Mexico, both adopted in the mid '60s, were accompanied by administrative decisions restricting legal immigration from Mexico into the United States even further. Since population growth in Mexico continued to outpace the ability of that country to produce new jobs, an increase in illegal immigration resulted. Prior to 1965, such illegality meant only that the individual had not followed through the administrative process of obtaining papers or had overstayed a temporary work permit. Now their very presence in this country places the immigrants outside the law.

The problem of those immigrants without proper entry permits has grown in the public mind in the last few years as economic conditions have deteriorated in America. A first concern is that of the numbers of people in this group. In 1971, then Attorney General William Saxbe warned the nation that there were probably one million people illegally in this country. By 1975, the then Commissioner of the Immigration and Naturalization Service, General Leonard Chapman—a former Marine Corps Commandant—alerted the annual convention of the American Legion to the "silent invasion" of illegal aliens who numbered about 12 million and threatened the very fabric of the American way of life.

Hispanics as a group have consistently called for a more compassionate immigration policy. They reject the term "illegal alien" on the grounds that a person cannot be illegal, only actions may be. They prefer the term "undocumented worker" to emphasize on the one hand the largely technical character of the legal infraction, and on the other the fact that most of these people are productive workers in the American labor market.

So far, Hispanics have been unsuccessful in changing public perceptions in America about the undocumented. Figures are still thrown about with abandon. And pictures of Mexicans attempting to cross the desolate border between Mexico and the United States are common in the papers. However the U.S. Bureau of the Census recently estimated the number of undocumented workers in this country at between 5 and 6 million. Even more surprising, the Census Bureau estimated that of those less than 60 percent were Mexican. The others were immigrants or visitors that had overstayed their legal entry permits.

Popular belief continues to hold that undocumented workers take away jobs from unemployed American citizens and legal residents and that they overburden public and social services. However research on the effect of undocumented workers on the labor market is inconclusive, with a serious line of thought maintaining that the undocumented workers enter what is called secondary labor markets where they are not in competition with American job-seekers. Furthermore, research consistently shows that although undocumented workers have taxes and Social Security contributions deducted from their pay checks some do not file income tax returns, frequently missing an opportunity to obtain tax refunds. Those workers are for the most part too afraid to take advantage of social services or public facilities that their taxes would legitimately provide for them.

The proposals of the Carter administration in 1977 attempted to solve the problem of the undocumented through a combination of measures: "amnesty" for those workers already in the country, according to two types of length of residence; penalties to the employers of undocumented workers; and unspecified assistance to Mexico to create new job opportunities that would ease the presure to emigrate.

Hispanics rejected these proposals. LULAC, IMAGE, the American G.I. Forum, and other Hispanic organizations felt that these proposals did not go far enough in creating a new immigration policy for the country. They felt that "amnesty" was not sufficient. But Hispanic leaders objected more strenuously to the aspects of the immigration reform package that decreed penalties for the employer of undocumented workers. Such penalties would require in their practical application a procedure for determining the legal status of a job applicant. The only viable way to accomplish this is through the issuance of a national counterfeit-proof work permit or national I.D.

This national I.D. card, necessary if employing un-documented workers is to be made effectively illegal, is viewed with horror by staunch conservatives. They argue that from such a card to a formal internal passport for all Americans is but a short step.

Hispanic leaders, such as Wilma Martinez, the director of the Mexican American Legal Defense and Education Fund (MALDEF), express a more personal concern over the I.D. card issue. Given the atmosphere of the country and the identification of undocumented worker with Mexicans, if a national I.D. card were issued only those individuals who "look" Mexican would be required to show it when applying for a job. In practice, the national work-permit or I.D. card would be a Mexican-American I.D. card.

These MALDEF fears are not unfounded. In spite of various administrative and judicial orders, immigration authorities and even police departments still detain and demand proof of residence or citizenship from people on the basis that the person "looks Mexican." If penalties are legislated for the employer of illegal aliens, many employers will want to avoid risks and will reject Hispanic job applicants out of hand. Race as a basic criterion to disqualify an applicant for a job would thus be encouraged by that legislation.

Immigration issues are complex, as are the "push" and "pull" factors that make citizens of Mexico and other countries look at the United States as a land of opportunities. International economic conditions, past policies, and the role of major American corporations abroad all continue to affect the issue of immigration, both legal and illegal. For Hispanics, these complex issues have "come home" in

a very personal way: It is the request for I.D. or birth
certificate or other kind of "papers" at the scene of a traffic
violation, at the door of the church after Sunday Mass, in
residential raids, or even at the park, when watching or
playing a soccer match.

At a political level, there is a line of thought about undocumented workers that is as dangerous to Hispanics as it
is subtle and unspoken. In 1975, for example, the Immigration Service estimated there were in the Chicago area
"about 500,000 illegal aliens, most of whom are Mexicans."
The U.S. Bureau of the Census, in reporting racial characteristics of the population, had identified fewer than
400,000 Hispanics of all national groups in the area, including Puerto Ricans, Texans, New Mexicans, and so
on—all American citizens by birth—as well as all legally
residing immigrants. The press dutifully published at various times both sets of figures, although they were obvi-
ously incompatible unless all Hispanics in the Chicago area
were "illegal." And that is precisely the policy impact of the
reasoning in much of the public consciousness. Mexican
Americans, Puerto Ricans, all Hispanics become identified
as aliens, even illegal aliens. The 1978 Census estimate of
the total number of Hispanics in the U.S. as 12 million is
the high figure for undocumented workers, "mostly Mexicans," that is popularly accepted.

Identification of Hispanics as aliens becomes as attractive as it is simplistic. The various social, economic, and
educational needs of Hispanics as a minority in the American society can be dismissed because as a group Hispanics
thus identified do not belong in America. Their political
demands would go away if only the country could seal its
borders effectively.

Under these circumstances, it may be easier to understand that immigration policies and public perception constitutes for many Hispanics a threshold question in the political arena. It is not necessarily because they or their families are affected by the immigration process, but because many Americans increasingly see Hispanics as the prototype of the alien. Any sense of belonging, in policy or government, by Hispanics is thus dismissed, as are any efforts at understanding or moving toward needed social and economic changes for this minority.

The leadership of the Catholic Church has shown a great deal of compassionate leadership on the issue of immigration. The teachings of Pope Pius XII in *Exsul Familia* were confirmed and emphasized by Paul VI in his instruction *Nemo Est*. The popes in fact have been so outspoken on this issue as to be revolutionary. They in fact have stated that the right of an individual to emigrate in search of freedom or a better life is a personal right that takes precedence even over the rights of countries to control access to their territory.

In the United States, bishops and other church leaders have consistently spoken out on the human rights of the immigrants, both in terms of national policy and the practice of advocating for individuals caught in the complexities of immigration law and procedures. The concern of the American hierarchy has been shown particularly for immigrants from Latin America, and is in fact often an extension of the concern they have for Latin America itself.

However, this joining of the two concerns has led to a futher subtle identification of Hispanics as aliens. In the church, this has meant the development of a "special" sort of church for Hispanics, unrelated to and tolerated by the mainstream hierarchical structure. One Hispanic priest expressed it this way: "Yes, the Archbishop sends us letters. We read them, but they have nothing to say to our people. They are not worth the effort to translate them for our parish. We simply throw them away." And he added, "The Archbishop does not know what we do in our parish, and he does not want to know as long as we send in our monthly parish assessment check on time. And as long as he leaves us alone to serve our people, this is all right with us. Those of us that serve Hispanics get together and are in touch. You could say we are a church apart."

8

Empowerment at the Grassroots

Political issues that overlap both the domestic and foreign areas, such as immigration or the status of Puerto Rico, are part of the political agenda of Hispanics in the United States. And there seems to be unusual agreement among Hispanic national groups on these issues. At a recent meeting of IMAGE, a group comprising mostly Mexican Americans, a resolution asking for the independence of Puerto Rico was the object of serious and heated debate. The Puerto Rican Legal Defense and Education Fund has demanded more humane immigration policies. Hispanic groups of every nationality have shown concern for the newly arrived Cubans.

The political demands of Hispanic groups relate to immediate domestic policies on a day to day basis. They are learning, as other marginated groups before them did, that the political arena is where social and economic conditions can be changed and living standards improved. The attempts these groups have made to influence political actions have varied widely throughout the country. Hispanics have not been able to build over the years the type of political and socio-political organizations that other minorities have built as focal points for their struggle. Lately, however, there have been stirrings that can be revolutionary in their long-range implications.

In recent years a new political force has emerged in San

Antonio. COPS (Community Organized for Public Service) is an umbrella group of organizations that in a short time has become an important element in city politics. COPS centers its actions on specific local issues. Then it mobilizes the community to pressure the authorities for specific actions, based on traditional Mexican American values of family and neighborhood networks. COPS in San Antonio began with the down-to-earth problem of sewers and drainage in the low-lying Hispanic barrios that were often subjected to periodic floods. It continued with social analyses and demands for allocation of various types of federal-city funds. Today COPS remains faithful to its own rule not to endorse a political candidate for office, nor to allow a COPS member to be a candidate while still an officer of the organization. But in San Antonio, no candidate for office would decline an invitation to appear before the collective leadership and members of COPS.

In the past, there have been groups in several American cities using techniques similar to those of COPS. In Chicago, the West Town Concerned Citizens Coalition, in the Puerto Rican barrio, achieved valuable affirmative action in employment gains for their people under the leadership of Rev. Jorge Morales, a Pentecostal minister.

What makes COPS distinctive is that as an umbrella group the great majority of its member organizations are Catholic parishes. Through this mechanism, the Catholic clergy and people have entered fully into the social action arena.

The example of COPS has started to spread. In California, a similar group has emerged in East Los Angeles under the name of UNO (United Neighborhood Organizations). The techniques are the same: careful study of complex local socio-economic issues; identification of the political powers that can effect a solution or change; and massive citizen action to move these political leaders to institute the necessary changes.

Again, Catholic parishes are the basic constituent organizations of the UNO umbrella group.

A local Chicano pastor in Los Angeles gave a simple explanation for the parish involvement in the activism of UNO: The parish has to survive. Housing deterioration, increase of crime, lack of basic public services would decimate the parish population as the neighborhood became less attractive to residents and families. So parishes must organize to improve local conditions if they hope to remain viable.

This explanation makes sense, but sells the new efforts short. Conditions were bad in the past, but there was no organized effort to do something about them. The movement by COPS and UNO is a new beginning, a new posture for the Catholic Church to side with Hispanics in action for social justice. If the movement and its techniques spread, there will be a new leadership emerging in the political arena at the local level where substantial changes can have national implication.

COPS and UNO are not the only church-fostered activities for the social progress of Hispanics, although they may be the most innovative. Traditional church operations, along the Catholic Charities model, work with and for Hispanics in many areas of the country.

Of particular relevance is the effort of the Campaign for Human Development. Sponsored by the U.S. Catholic Conference, the Campaign obtains its funds from an annual Sunday church collection and distributes them to local projects, selected and administered by the local diocese, and to national projects carried out the CHD staff.

In 1979, the Campaign distributed approximately $6 million for national projects, and of that sum about $1.5 million went to projects serving mostly Hispanics. From 1976 to 1979, the Campaign has funded over 50 projects for Hispanics nationwide, in depressed rural areas and inner cities. There is no similar information about diocesan-administered projects, but the effort at the national level has been consistently sensitive to the needs of Hispanics to an extent that not many private philanthropies or government programs can remotely match.

Among the projects funded by the national Campaign, the one at Providence of God Church in the Chicago Mexican American barrio of Pilsen acquired national prominence when Pope John Paul II in his 1979 visit to the United States stopped at its doors and addressed the crowd in Spanish. Other projects include the Center for Social Services for Hispanics in Lorain, Ohio; the Texas Agricultural Labor Relations Project of the Texas Farmworkers Union in San Juan, Texas; contributions to both COPS and UNO; the Peoples' Advocate Consortium in Greeley, Colorado; the Northeast Pastoral Center in New York; legal services in California, Texas, and Colorado; radio programs in California and Colorado; housing developments in California, New York, New Jersey, and Connecticut; voter registration in Texas; economic development projects in Texas and California, and so on.

Nor are grant-making activities the only evidence of concern by the Campaign for Human Development with Hispanics. Hispanics have been brought into the citizens' committees that make the grant decisions, both at national and regional levels.

Most of these projects have one thing in common: they may be involved in providing services to the individuals and communities, but for the most part they are in the business of change. And in that respect they have a political relevance, either as training and support bases for leadership, or as "seed" projects to secure other private or federal funds for community improvement.

The policy of the Campaign staff has not gone unnoticed. Hispanic leaders and media have consistently praised the effort. And some strong voices within the American church have been raised to denounce the political nature of some of the grant-making activities of the Campaign. Those voices, representing powerful members of that hierarchy, will probably have a final say on whether the innovative policies of the Campaign for Human Development continue and improve in the future.

* * *

Hispanics have joined the political process in various ways. In the recent past, some political groups have operated outside the conventional party process. In the '60s, there were a variety of revolutionary groups, such as the Green Berets in California and the Midwest among Chicanos, or the Mexican American Youth Organization, and the Chicano Student Movement of Aztlán. Among Puerto Ricans, the best known group of that era was the Young Lords Party, started in Chicago and eventually expanded to New York. Most of these movements have today largely disappeared.

Taking a different approach, and lacking the rigid, for the most part Marxist, ideology of those revolutionary movements, but also outside of the American political mainstream, was the *La Raza Unida* Party in Texas. Angel González, its best-known leader, centered on local issues and managed a victory in Crystal City, Texas that gave the party first the control over the school board and then over the city council itself, in a city where there had always existed a majority of Mexican American population together with a total lack of political power. *La Raza Unida* at one point was able to also field state-wide candidates for office in Texas and showed promise of substantial changes in the political role of Mexican Americans in that state. That promise has today been largely forgotten.

Political involvement of Hispanics in conventional party politics in America has led them to join in the complex coalitions that have traditionally made up the Democratic Party. Economic and social issues of most concern to Hispanics have more often found expression in the Democratic Party platforms. A more formal involvement of Hispanics in the Democratic Party occurred in the 1960 presidential campaign when "Viva Kennedy" clubs sprang up in most of the Hispanic Southwest. (One major factor in the Kennedy following in those areas had to do with the candidate's Catholicism.) Voting at that time by Hispanics carried substantial weight as a swing factor in several states and was a component of the Kennedy victory.

President Lyndon B. Johnson began to bring special attention of the federal government to Hispanics at the national level, with the creation of the Mexican American Inter-Agency Committee in the late '60s. The Republican administration of President Nixon upgraded that effort by the creation of the congressionally mandated Cabinet Committee on Opportunities for the Spanish–Speaking in 1970. The partisan politics of that committee at the time of the Nixon re-election campaign in 1972 led to its demise when it came up for an extension in 1974.

But by that time the presence of Hispanics and the need to involve them not only in the electioneering process (both parties created special Hispanic campaigns in 1972, 1976, and 1980) but also in the national government processes had been established as a bipartisan policy.

Federal programs to increase employment of Hispanics in government were initiated in 1970 as a component of the Equal Employment Opportunity policy of the government's Office of Personnel Management and the various departments and agencies. And the accepted presidential policy included appointment of Hispanics to high government positions. Presidents Johnson, Nixon, and Carter have successively outdone each other in this process. This phenomenon has given rise to a new, more visible Hispanic leadership on the national scene. Similar actions are slowly being taken at state levels, where governors' committees or legislative commissions are being created with the particular mandate to advocate for Hispanics at the state government level.

Some Hispanics express skepticism about the true leadership role of this growing number of appointees. Emphasizing that they occupy nonelective positions for the most part, critics see these emerging leaders as establishment-bound, chosen by the real powers who are strangers to the Hispanic communities, and placed in high positions because of their acceptance of the majority order. Their subsequent docility makes them no threat to that established order.

The criticism makes sense, and the danger is real. But the presence of Hispanics in positions of political power, even if those positions are limited by their appointive character, is in itself a new, progressive development towards the political empowerment of Hispanic communities across the country. Ideally, it will lead to the real power that comes from elective office leadership.

9

The Language Issue

A domestic issue that has captured the imagination of Hispanics and national groups across the country is bilingual education.

Bilingual education, like many educational issues, is as much a political as an educational concern. It broke into the political consciousness of the country in 1967 with the passage by Congress of the Bilingual Education Act, Title VII of the Elementary and Secondary Education Act of 1965, one of the key legislative building blocks of President Johnson's Great Society initiatives.

The original bill for bilingual education was the idea of Mexican American educators and politicians in Texas. Senator Ralph Yarborough introduced the bill and managed it through Congress over the opposition of the U.S. Office of Education, representing the administration position. Passage of the bill into law was secured by the compassionate national response to the plight of the newly arrived Cubans in Dade County, Florida in the middle '60s.

The Bilingual Education Act of 1967 offered no description of bilingual education. It authorized the federal government to make grants to school districts to establish bilingual education programs. Only the 1974 Education Amendments, which revamped the Bilingual Education Act, would define the concept and educational practice. In the meantime, and in spite of the minimal size of the federal appropriations, Hispanics across the country had rallied around the concept and policy of bilingual education and had started to forge coalitions with other language minority groups to increase the importance of and allocations for this new program.

In 1971, the state of Illinois appropriated $210,000 for bilingual education programs in the Chicago public schools. It was the first state to commit its own funds to the concept. In 1972, Massachussetts passed legislation mandating bilingual education in schools where a minimum of 20 pupils came from homes using languages other than English. In the following years other states followed this lead: Texas, Wisconsin, Michigan, California, and others mandated bilingual education, making state funds available to carry out such programs.

The bilingual education movement was growing, and it was bolstered further by the Supreme Court of the United States in the landmark case of *Lau vs. Nichols* in 1974. Lau was a young Chinese student, on whose behalf the San Francisco School Board was sued with a demand that special assistance in acquiring English language skills be given to Lau and other Chinese-speaking students.

The Board of Education countered that San Francisco schools were providing those children with the same services given to other children and that the Board of Education could not be made responsible for remedying an English deficiency that Chinese-speaking children brought into the classroom which prevented them from taking full advantage of the educational programs offered by the schools to every pupil. The U.S. District Court and eventually the Appeals Court both agreed with the board's position.

The Supreme Court unanimously reversed the lower

courts, and in its decision held that teaching of English was a primary function of the school system. To demand mastery of such language before the school could teach it to the students was to "make a mockery of public education." Equality of educational opportunity was not achieved by offering the same instructional program and resources to English-speaking and Chinese-speaking pupils. The court did not determine what specific programs the San Francisco school system was to offer the students, limiting themselves to affirming that such programs were necessary and mandatory. Advocates of bilingual education have insisted that this approach is the only way for effective teaching of the non-English-speaking pupil. Hispanics have been the primary beneficiaries, and Hispanic educators the strongest defenders of bilingual education.

Bilingual education remains highly controversial. In the summer of 1980, the newly established U.S. Department of Education published proposed guidelines, making bilingual education mandatory for school districts with sizable populations of non-English-speaking pupils, as the best implementation of the need for educational equality in opportunities defined by the *Lau* case.

The opposition to bilingual education became loud and strong. Established education lobby groups, such as the National Association of School Boards, state school officials, and several teachers' unions publicly decried the attempts by the federal government to mandate modes of instruction to the state and local school authorities. That federal interference with state and local decisions was the heart of the opposition is reminiscent of the "states rights" arguments that had been used to oppose desegregation and other federal civil rights mandates of the past.

117

The Browning of America

The question of bilingualism and the use of language other than English in the classroom has been an emotional issue in America throughout history. Non-English-speaking groups have been the target of prejudiced sentiment for many years. Beginning in 1889 and culminating at the time of World War I, 37 states had passed legislation restricting the use and even the teaching of languages other than English in the classroom before high school. Nor was this prohibition limited to public schools: it included Catholic and other private schools as well, as in the case of the German language schools in Wisconsin and the Japanese language schools in Hawaii and California. One of the necessary tasks for the modern-day proponents of bilingual education has been the repeal of such state legislation, and they have succeeded in making it obsolete or unenforced in most states.

But the opposition to bilingual education continues, with a variety of arguments. They run from the reasoning that "other immigrants made it without special programs," to the fear that encouraging bilingualism could increase separatism and "Quebec-ization" of the United States. The present mood of the country to reduce public tax expenditures, exemplified by California's "Proposition 13," has increased the public questioning of expenditures in any social programs; bilingual education has been opposed as a social program benefiting for the most part Hispanic children of low economic levels.

As the controversy rages, both on economic and ideological grounds, one may want to examine what there is about bilingual education that elicits such an emotional response. The term can be interpreted in several ways. In a purely academic context, it could be defined as an instructional program aimed at producing a person who knows two languages. The question in America today is by no means purely academic. In the current American school practice, all mandated or authorized bilingual education is *transitional*. It has a much more limited purpose than to create or preserve bilingualism in the pupil. Instead, the goal is to make the pupil a fluent speaker of English. The program is bilingual in that to achieve that end it uses the language that the child brings into the classroom, instead of only English that is unintelligible to the pupil.

In this context, bilingual education is pupil-centered, rather than school-oriented. Five-year-old Juan Lopez, coming to kindergarten speaking only Spanish, will be met by a teacher who knows Spanish and will be taught English. While he learns the new language, he will be able to communicate with the teacher and will learn other subject matters, such as math, social science, and so on, in the language he is more comfortable with. By the time he has completed two or three years of school, he will have learned English well and will have kept pace with other students in the other areas of learning. And nowhere in the course of the school experience will Juan have been told that speaking Spanish is no good, nor will he be penalized for speaking Spanish, and he will not have to be ashamed of his Spanish-speaking parents.

The issue of bilingual education, thus described, is as political as it is educational. In the simplicity of using Spanish, the language of the child, there is more than a change in instructional tools. Bilingual education recognizes the diversity of the student and accepts the fact that the pupil is not just deficient in English, but is a speaker of another language, a legitimate mode of expression worth using in the very process of teaching English.

Hispanics see in this recognition more than an educational breakthrough. The more schools stop equating Spanish with lack of English and accept it simply as a different language the less likely will it be that Hispanic pupils will be confined to mentally–retarded classrooms because of English language tests; the more schools communicate with parents, the less likely that the Hispanic pupil will feel alienated and out of place in the school.

So bilingual education represents a new era. It is the beginning of the end of rejection of Spanish language and the cultural implications and identity that goes with it. At its heart, it has the potential for ending the basic discrimination against this minority group in the nation's public schools.

This potential is the basis for the emotional commitment of Hispanics to bilingual education. Compared to this basic identity issue, other reasons to support bilingual education may seem to carry a lesser weight. There seems to be scholarly evidence that acquisition of reading skills is easier in a second language (English) after they have first mastered the native tongue (Spanish). Progress in math, social studies, and other academic subjects is faster in a bilingual than in a monolingual classroom for non-English speakers, and so on. There are other political reasons, although not perhaps of the same urgency: In a world of increasing national interdependence, it is an asset for the United States to preserve and cultivate people who can communicate across national borders in languages other than English.

Puerto Ricans could propose a different kind of argument for bilingual education. As American citizens, they are entitled to the freedom to come and go between the island and the continental United States. For them, growing up bilingual may be considered vital in the exercise of that freedom of movement and residence, at least as long as Puerto Rico retains Spanish as its official language.

Loyalty to a culture is at the root of the bilingual education controversy. Underneath the conflicting arguments, there is the attachment of the individual to a language as an expression of culture and assertion of personal as well as collective identity.

The Catholic Church, in relating to Hispanics, has been affected by the cultural and language yearnings of this minority. As in many other instances, the response that the organized church has given can be characterized as mixed.

The Catholic Church experienced a language revolution of her own as a consequence of Vatican Council II, with the abandoning of Latin as the language of worship and adoption of the vernacular instead. Only after that basic change could the question of what vernacular to use come to the forefront. English was universally established in the United States. Then other languages began to be used as the congregations made their needs known. Today it is quite common for churches with a Hispanic population to use Spanish as the language of worship. Perhaps nowhere in the response of the American church to the needs of Hispanics has there been as much emphasis as in the learning and using of Spanish at church functions.

American bishops, with no great numbers of native Spanish-speaking priests, sent priests to Puerto Rico or to Cuernavaca, Mexico for special language instruction, or to other Latin American countries on assignments that mixed missionary ministries and language learning internships.

Spanish has been fully accepted as a language of worship, but not without friction. As the worship became less formal after Vatican II, guitars substituted for organs and basements for the main church. In many churches, the Spanish Mass was confined to the basement, and Hispanic parishioners were in fact banished from the main church. But in parishes where Hispanics are numerous and have the privilege of Hispanic or bilingual clergy, the vitality of the theological understandings has been embodied in an explosion of new liturgical expressions. New music, new prayers, full acceptance of melodies and musical instruments from the heart of Hispanic cultural traditions have placed Spanish at the center of the worship service, of which the homily is just an added element.

The resulting liturgical revival has astounded the rest of the American church. When the annual bishops conference gathered in Chicago in the spring of 1980, their concelebrated Mass at St. Francis of Assisi, a Mexican barrio church, was the liturgical highlight of the three-day meeting. The beauty and joy of the newly evolved liturgy of American Hispanics is seen by many church leaders as a major contribution of this minority to the total American church.

However, acceptance of the language of the Hispanics has been confined to the realm of worship. Catholic schools remain by and large monolingual. Catholic education has succeeded in staying substantially at the margin of the bilingual education movement for Hispanics in the United States.

Hispanic parents often choose Catholic schools for their

children for many reasons, from religious interest to the awareness that parish-school pupils achieve better than those in the inner-city public schools. For many of these families, tuition to the parochial school represents a significant financial commitment. Only families who put a high value on education will take on that financial burden.

As of the fall of 1979, 248,500 Hispanic students attended Catholic elementary and secondary schools, representing 8 percent of the total pupil population, an increase from 5 percent in 1970–1971. Figures for individual diocesan schools are not available, but of course the Hispanic pupils are not distributed uniformly through all schools in the country. Partial data show that in the Archdiocese of Los Angeles the elementary parochial schools enroll 32,075 pupils, 42.5 percent of the total. Chicago Catholic schools have seen their Hispanic enrollment grow from 5 percent in 1970 to 10 percent in 1979–1980. The Archdiocese of New York lists 22,452 Hispanics (23 percent of the total) in its elementary schools, and 6,056 (15.1 percent of the total) in its high schools. In some of the New York areas, Hispanics represent the largest ethnic group in the schools. In Manhattan, for instance, they make up 47.9 percent of the pupil population.

Even with this substantial presence of Hispanics in American Catholic schools, bilingual education has not made an impact. Parish schools continue to be monolingual in English, with very few exceptions. This monolingualism of the schools is another example of the prevalence of "Americanization" over "evangelization" as the goal of the American church with respect to Hispanics today.

Many leaders, both in and out of the church structure,

will make bilingual education a political demand from federal and state and local governments, but will not demand it from Catholic schools. The cost of this educational approach and the relative rate of success of Catholic schools as they are are given as arguments not to push bilingual education for Hispanic children in parochial schools.

And yet there is a strong tradition of bilingualism in the history of Catholic education in most major cities of the Eastern and Midwestern United States. As an extension of the national parish, education in the parochial school for Germans, Poles, and Italians was often bilingual, even after the public schools banned non-English languages from the classrooms at the time of World War I. Such bilingual schools could still be found in the ethnic central-city schools as late as the early '60s. English as well as the native language were accepted languages of instruction in those classrooms.

These bilingual schools have disappeared as the white ethnic populations have ceased to be majorities in the central cities. But Catholic schools have not picked up Spanish as the new "target" language as more and more Hispanic pupils have enrolled there. The role of the Catholic Church and parochial school in the social progress of ethnic minorities has not been resumed with the Hispanic migrations. The schools have not taken up this challenge with the same historical success that they did in the old bilingual schools.

There are other political implications in bilingual education in the nation's public schools. In the inner city, where Hispanics often share with blacks the largest proportion of pupil enrollments, bilingual education has been seen by some as a threat to pupil desegregation. From a superficial viewpoint, there is an initial appearance of contradiction between these two requirements for educational equality. Desegregation aims at breaking up the isolation of black students in schools of their own, at times requiring the transporting of pupils across neighborhoods to achieve an integration of pupils from various racial backgrounds. On the other hand, bilingual education programs may require the concentration of pupils from non-English-speaking backgrounds, so that the numbers may make the programs administratively viable.

The two sets of requirements are conceptually easy to reconcile, as both of them stem from a basic effort to provide equality of educational opportunities to minority pupils who would not have them otherwise. But in individual school districts, as the complex plans are developed, friction between the black and Hispanic communities might be generated at a high emotional level.

Conflict between black and Hispanic minorities can be frequent at the grassroot level. Hispanics share in racial prejudices, and blacks at times resent the attention given to Hispanics who are not black. Bilingual education programs are manifestations of attention that may be resented; so are negative feelings about undocumented workers, said to take away from poor blacks jobs that are already scarce. Hispanics complain that black leadership will use Hispanic demographics and organization support to obtain concessions for minorities in programs that when set in place favor only blacks.

One particularly difficult black-Hispanic conflict in 1980 was the rioting and destruction at Liberty City in Florida, touched off by the acquittal of a group of policemen accused of killing a black man. Resentment had accumulated for a long time before the summer explosion, and part of the resentment was directed at the seemingly prosperous Hispanic-Cuban community in the area.

These sporadic frictions have a common air of hopelessness about them. After all, the arguments occur between powerless groups, neither of which has much to gain from the dispute. It is fortunate when the leadership of both minorities actively seeks cooperation and meaningful coalitions between them.

10

Is It a Question of Time?

The banal story is true enough. A young man, a recent arrival from Spain, was trying to understand a fine point of American social habits. His friends were expressing their distrust for blacks, Puerto Ricans, Mexicans .... At one point, the young man turned to his companions and asked: "But I am Spanish. I have been here in the States only one year, and you accepted me from the very first day." "Yes," was the reply, "you spoke Spanish, but we knew you came from Spain. You were not Puerto Rican or Mexican." "Would you have treated me differently if you knew I was Puerto Rican?" "You bet."

The episode is not uplifting, and it forces the consideration of a painful reality that needs to be faced when discussing Hispanics in the United States. It is true that numerically the bulk of the Hispanics constitute new arrivals in the long tradition of immigration to America. As they speak a non-English language, they occupy the bottom of the economic and social ladder. It would seem they are going through the same process that previous European immigrants endured before them. And one may ask: Is it a question of time? Will Hispanics also make it in America, the same way that Germans, Italians, Poles, or Greeks before them?

The question is not of purely historical, speculative interest. It has immediate policy implications. If the answer is yes, there is no need for bilingual education programs (that previous immigrants supposedly did not have) and no need for special affirmative action efforts to secure equal employment or educational opportunities for Hispanics. If they are like previous immigrants, their first generation will endure hard times, but their children will make it. If European immigrants succeeded, why not Hispanics?

There are of course historical differences. The bulk of the Puerto Rican arrivals to the continental United States occurred between 1940 and 1965. The country was quite different then from what it was in the 19th century. What characterized the early, European arrivals—"a strong back and a willingness to work"—were also qualities that Puerto Rican migrants possessed to a large degree. But the country they found was now a technological society, and the newcomers' lack of education and technical skills handicapped them in a way that it had not previous immigrants. As Samuel Betances put it: "We brought along our cane-cutting *machetes,* but what was needed was skills in running computers!" In the same line, when Mexican Americans worked their way north from Texas to the Minnesota fields, they, unlike their European immigrant predecessors, could not settle on the land. The time of homesteading in an ever-expanding territory had passed.

These historical explanations point to differences between Hispanics and previous immigrant groups. But they are not sufficient, and there is a more basic distinction. The underlying premise of the comparison with the experience of previous immigrants is that there is an open-ended, evolutionary process whereby the immigrant will succeed in America as a group after a generation or two of poverty and hard work. Current social status of an immigrant group, therefore, would be dependent on the length of time since arrival and can be considered as just a stage in the assimilative process.

The premise and the process—basically the dynamics of the "melting pot"—have not worked with a very conspicuous ethnic group: the American blacks. They arrived in America before most European immigrants. They even gained legal freedom from slavery before the bulk of non-English European immigration took place, in the late 19th and early 20th centuries. And yet they remain at the bottom of the ladder. Historical group "seniority," assumed to be determinant of the group success, does not work in the case of blacks. The melting pot was never meant for blacks.

Nor has it been meant for American Indians or for Hispanics. "Mexicans" were already in the country that became America in 1848 after the Treaty of Guadalupe Hidalgo. And Puerto Ricans began to live in American territory, their own island, in 1898 after the Spanish American War. They have made no progress comparable to European immigrants.

In the last 25 years, as the country has become more aware of the demands for equality, legislation and social mores have focused on minorities and have insisted on their need for full civil rights.

In a sense, everybody in America is a member of a minority group. And as national groups have become more assertive of their ethnic identity, some of them would define themselves as minorities, threatening to cause bureaucratic classificational nightmares.

One way to make the term "minority" better understood in its sociological and legal implications may be to define it differently. Minority of course means a group identifiable as a "minor" demographic component of a population such as the United States. But minorities in America today could interpret that name as derived from "minor," as in a minor in age. Their main characteristic is not so much that they are a smaller group in the total population—in many cities, blacks or Hispanics are now the numerical majority, as they are in many schools. Rather, it is the fact that their human and civil rights resemble in practice those of a minor. They are incomplete and limited.

Unlike a minor in age, the members of these minority groups are confined to this limited enjoyment of rights on a permanent basis. Discrimination is the cause and framework of those limitations. Minority groups that would fit this understanding share common traits: their historical arrival into American society, unlike that of the European immigrants, was not voluntary. Blacks came as slaves; Puerto Ricans became a part of America as the result of negotiations between the United States and Spain in faraway Paris after the Spanish American war and without a formal consultation with the inhabitants of the island. What today is the Southwest United States became America as a result of war and subsequent treaty agreements.

But the most obvious common trait of minorities in America as defined here is a racial characteristic: they all are nonwhite and as such easily identifiable. In this sense, Hispanics are closer to blacks as a racially discriminated–against group than they are to European immigrants: Hispanics are ethnics, but they are also a racial minority in America. In the days of the early European immigration, it was common for individuals from a less desirable national group to change names. A Scalabrini or a Kucinski by changing their names to Smith could evade the major impact of their pejorative identification. Today we abhor such societal pressures, but at the time they represented avenues of escape and swifter assimilation into American society. For many Hispanics, a change of name will make them no more acceptable: A González by any other name still is identifiable racially as a Mexican.

This racial characterization also typifies the major difference between minority groups and the current emphasis on "Euro-ethnic" identity. White ethnicity has been defined here as optional, requiring a positive decision of the individual to seek and retain his/her cultural tradition and identity. For Hispanics and for blacks and other racial minorities, this identification is mandatory to a large extent and is imposed from the outside by a society that places an overwhelming value on being white.

Recently some students of the personality have developed a model to explain the implications of this phenomenon. They have called their explanation the *dual perspective*. According to them, a person develops first in an intimate circle made up of family and others similarly close. The nurturing functions of that circle allow the individual's personality to grow. At a point, this initial circle expands into a wider environment: school, media, work. Each of these two circles provides a perspective for the progressive development of the growing person.

However, while for the racial–majority individual the larger circle confirms and strengthens the growth fostered by the narrower initial environment, the minority person discovers that the wider circle negates his or her closer, intimate environment. In fact, that majority environment specifically rejects the minority characteristics of that individual. There is indeed a dual perspective in which society

131

at large counteracts the effects of the inner circle through discrimination. So while a majority-group person grows from an inner circle perspective into a wider perspective, a major task of the minority individual is to synthesize the antagonism between the two perspectives which he or she is exposed to.

The conclusion seems inescapable. For Hispanics, as for blacks, the American church structure seems to be today a part of that second, conflicting wider environment that rejects the Hispanic individual on the basis of race.

In terms of church policy, the path to overcome the dual perspective conflict can only lead through a deep theological understanding. The situation of a group, rejected by society, confined to a minority situation, seems to be made to order for a full actualization of the church's gospel message. It is the role of the church to seek out and align itself with the poor, the rejected, the marginated. American society could be said to have institutionalized this process of rejection through racial identification and discrimination. By doing so, it has constrained the church to only one possible position—that of fulfilling its mission of "evangelizing the poor."

Seen in that light, the Hispanics, far from representing a problem to be solved, constitute a reason-for-being for the church in America today, as do other racial and ethnic minorities. They represent the future of the church, if it finds in itself the strength to be faithful to that, its crucial mission.

11

A New Doctrine:
The Theology of Liberation

When Pope John Paul traveled to Mexico in 1979, the Catholic Church in Latin America held its breath. The Pope's visit was not purely ceremonial, although hundreds of thousands would welcome the pilgrim Pontiff and strive for a glimpse of his "Popemobile." The Pope was also to meet in Mexico with the Latin American church hierarchy in episcopal conference, the CELAM, gathered for a special session. And he could be presented, for the first time in his pontificate, with the dilemma that has been the major concern of the Latin American church for the last 20 years: the divisive interpretation of the role of the church in a world beset with social problems. At the base was the question of whether that church should choose sides in a society divided in regard to the owning of means of production.

The ferment of social change in a social context has not been limited to Latin America. In France, there was the priest-worker movement in the '50s and the underlying theology of *engagement*—the commitment of the priest and layperson to a temporal world, not just in a vertical line of private God-human relationships relevant to an after-life alone. In Italy, this ferment was epitomized by the movement that adopted the name of *aggiornamento* and called into question the relationship of the commited Christian to the political system. It posed the dilemma of the professed

Catholic faced with a choice of voting for a political party ideologically atheistic but pragmatically attractive in that its platform stressed equality over property and unequal rights.

In Latin America, the movement in the last 20 years has been intensive, and has centered on the role of the church with respect to the poor. The Latin American church, to a degree unparalleled in other areas of the world, has buttressed social action concerns and programs with a new, profound political analysis: the so-called "theology of liberation."

For many, this theology is not a new exploration of old truths or a particular emphasis and insight into specific aspects of revelation. The theology of liberation is for them a new methodology—such a different way of looking at theology that it changes the very concept of theological thinking, making other styles obsolete.

It is not possible to describe fully the tenets of the theology of liberation in a short summary. Some ideas may help in understanding the major concepts prevalent today in the Latin American theological thought.

Avery Dulles has identified three aspects of faith: fiduciary—trust in God; intellectualist—belief in a set of truths; and performative—the active engagement in "the historical praxis of liberation." This last characterizes the new thought. In this conception of the world, there is the understanding that Christ reveals himself continuously through the mediation of history and the conviction that history is a dialectic of institutions engaged in battle over the ownership and control of the means of production, rather than the result of individual actions that deviate more or less from a set of ethical demands.

The Theology of Liberation

Latin American itself must be the beginning of the exploration of the theology of liberation. A vast area, both geographically and demographically, the subcontinent has in common not only language and cultural background and traditions, but also a common set of social and economic conditions. Latin America is rich in raw materials and depends for manufactured goods and heavy industry on the major industrialized nations of the world, particularly the United States. As a result, most of the nations in Latin America can be called underdeveloped or developing countries.

The wealth in Latin America is so unevenly distributed that a minority of rich individuals, either landowners or chiefs of industry or business, live in a luxury unknown to many heavily-taxed wealthy people in other countries, while the vast majority of Latin Americans are subject to economic conditions where they may be still in the bartering era, outside a currency economy. This is the massive group that has been described as *marginated,* not only outside the economic mainstream, but as a consequence also outside any meaningful political participation.

Under these economic conditions, the democratic character of most of the Latin American nations is often a thin veneer, and the ground is fertile for dictatorships, the historical bane of Latin America. Latin America thus offers a most appropriate climate for socialism. Marx, the founder of Marxist communism, made a cornerstone of his theory the fact that socialism was the natural result of the conflict over the means of production. Accordingly socialism could best develop first in the most highly industrialized nations of the world, mostly in Western Europe. Historically that process did not take place, and it was left to Lenin to restructure the theoretical underpinnings of socialism, to make it—and its accompanying dictatorship of the proletariat—particularly suited for underdeveloped countries. In Russia, China, and later in Cuba, it was expected that socialism would leapfrog the process of economic development. Through a tight control of the means of production, underdeveloped countries would be able to create the infrastructures that would allow nations to achieve the proper level of technological and economic development.

Socialism as the solution to the national underdevelopment became a most attractive alternative for Latin America. The first socialist regime occurred in Cuba. And Latin America witnessed the first instance in the world of a communist government brought about by popular election and not violent revolution: the Salvador Allende regime in Chile.

The ideology of socialist revolution spread through Latin America with an enthusiasm that made Ché Guevara an international hero. Young priests, some of them from Spain, were torn between the traditional teachings of the church and their honest empathy for the poor, for whom the revolution seemed to be a better way to a new era of equality. For the first time in modern history, priests sided openly with the revolutionaries, and some of them gave their lives in the course of violent revolution.

The structured church also was facing the choice between the continued acceptance of the status quo, or a reorientation to the service of the poor, the marginated. Many young priests and lay people took a definite position. Even while not taken up in violent revolution, they sided with the left for social justice, with those who envisioned a new era where social classes would be closer. For them, this posture was a return to basic teachings of their faith—to serve the poor as Christ himself had done.

In this struggle, political parties modeled after European movements, such as Christian Democrats, were found wanting for the task at hand. And out of the new orientation to social justice the gospel message of faith and the socialist ideology concurred in goals and urgency. The theology of liberation was born to give a theological underpinning to the new socio-pastoral alignments.

The theology of liberation borrowed perspectives from Marxism. The traditional intellectualistic or fiduciary faith was loaded with idealistic, dogmatic tenets and proposed a moral code that failed to incorporate behavior into the faith commitment. The consequence was that personal departure from Christian teachings was pictured as the sole cause of injustice, while for the oppressed patience and a hope for afterlife happiness substituted for action in search for active justice.

The new theology accepted a factual—some will call it a materialistic—interpretation of history. History in this dialectical interpretation is not necessarily a parallel set of developments: on one plane the theory and ethical code, and on the other the reality where those moral codes fail to bring about justice and equality. History is but an evolution of means of production. If so, one must look to what exists structurally in society and not through an examination of individual aberrations from a moral ideal. And social conditions do not result from, but create, the set of moral values a society lives by at any given historical moment.

In practice, then, church preachings that encourage patience, the call for resignation to unjust conditions, are the ideological expression appropriate to a time in the evolution of the economic and class struggle where it was vital for those in control of the means of production to delay the historical process on their own behalf. The main ethical demand of the theology of liberation is the understanding of this process and the realization that revelation occurs mediated by history. The faith commitment implies acceptance and praxis in the direction of the "right" evolutionary way. Liberation, a term with deep theological and biblical connotations, comes in the conscious awareness of that direction, and the giving of oneself to the change that must come. The commitment then is expressed by conscientization, the growing awareness and the implacable analysis of society to identify what is the next step towards the ultimate end of an equalitarian control of the means of production.

In this context, a church moved by the theology of liberation is an ally of revolutionary, even socialistic forces, rather than their staunchest ideological foe. Liberating action, in light of the task ahead, takes precedence over differing interpretations of abstract dogma. Even negation of a transcendent God, as demanded by communism, or the acceptance of God's message, are of less immediate concern. Action is the expression of faith, and allies in the struggle are less questioned in their ideological posture than welcomed in the pursuit of the common goals.

There are theoretical roadblocks to a full development of a theology of liberation, even though its main ideas are attractive on their face, since they put justice ahead of private, behavior-unrelated beliefs. The most important of these roadblocks is perhaps precisely the redundancy of a role for a transcendent divinity who chose to intervene freely in the course of human history, and whose intervention negates the basic analysis of history as evolution of control over the means of production in a deterministic class struggle.

More than this, a theology of liberation leaves too little room for human frailty and dismisses too easily the possibility of failure by individuals in their otherwise honest attempt at commitment. It may be that it is difficult for a rich person to enter the kingdom of heaven, but Jesus never denied the possibility. The theology of liberation, with its ideological debt to socialism, represents such a drastic departure from traditional thought that it is often rejected out of hand. And yet the theology of liberation may be the best meeting ground for Christianity and progressive social forces, including the socialists, in a world where socialism is the accepted way of thought and life for so many.

In the last instance, those who criticize the theology of liberation for its socialistic tones are faced with the identification of their own theology with the only other economic system, capitalism. And this system, not as it should be or could be in an ideal world but as practiced today, often amounts to the exploitation of the many by a few. Collective control of the means of production does not on the face of it seem any more contrary to the gospel than protection of individual private property.

Whatever the final judgment on theology of liberation, its intellectual vitality is only one ideological expression of the prevalent attitude in Latin American churches today: the reorientation of religious leadership to social justice as an immediate goal calling for action, without taking shelter from its demands in the expectation of a more just after-life. While the specific intellectual path to theology of liberation may not be accepted by many in Latin America, this reorientation as the ultimate expression of the Christian message is well on its way to becoming the normal priority of the church in El Salvador, Nicaragua, Costa Rica, Colombia, and many other Latin American countries.

This reorientation, with the conscientization and re-alignment implied, is also the accepted line of thought for the Hispanic church in the United States. Among the clergy, there has been a solid understanding and progress in liberation theology. To the extent that Hispanics constitute in the United States a minority socially and politically marginated, the historical analysis advanced by liberation theology explains and encourages the role of a Hispanic church, with a commitment to social justice and a new order, through responsible political activism. This commitment does not depend on acceptance of each and every one of the steps proposed by the theologians of liberation. But to the extent that the mainstream American church has other objectives, Hispanics and their clergy cannot relate to it.

This is not to say that Hispanics are asking their American church to take a political stand and thus break with the tradition of the separation of church and politics in America. They insist that the American church is already a political force. The efforts of the church in the political realm on behalf of abortion policies or a change in state support for private Catholic schools, for instance, are seen as proof of an existing political involvement of the church. What they demand is a reorientation of the uses of that political power to issues relating to Hispanics as poor, and in need of social justice.

12

Hispanics Are Here to Stay. Or Are They?

The General Secretary of the National Conference of Catholic Bishops agreed to discuss Hispanics in the American church. In very friendly terms, he took time from his schedule and privately reflected on their character and needs. He himself has a distinguished history of helping increase concern for Hispanics in the American church, developing structures and services for them.

Then he was asked: "What are your plans, the plans of the Catholic hierarchy, for Hispanics in the future?" The prelate took a long moment to reflect. Then he threw up his hands, concerned and puzzled at the same time: "Plans? That is a very good question. I do not think I have an answer for you. Let me think the question over. Maybe at some other time I can have a proper answer . . . ."

The Bishop's reaction was as candid as it was pastorally concerned, and maybe it only reflected a desire not to give an incomplete off-the-cuff response, taking instead a committed, reflected-upon posture. Nevertheless, the answer was symptomatic of the present status of Hispanics in the American church. There is a gap between the faithful who continue to attend church services, however irregularly, and try to pattern their lives according to the Catholic faith, and a church that continues not to know what to make of them.

It is not that the church ignores Hispanics. As mentioned earlier, the Campaign for Human Development in 1979 allocated one-third of its available funds to Hispanic-oriented projects. Catholic schools, while remaining on the margin of the bilingual education movement, continue to provide an education superior to that of the public schools to an increasing number of Hispanic pupils. Catholic Charities throughout the country provide services to Hispanic poor, from immigration assistance to shelter for runaway children.

Perhaps the clues to the gap between American church institutions and Hispanics lie in this emphasis on services. Traditional as it may be, provision of services alone cannot be a substitute for engaging in change. Except for the couple of efforts described before—COPS and UNO—the American church has not joined Hispanics in their struggle for change in social conditions. Services are good, but there is also the need for political empowerment, decreased discrimination, affirmative action, liberation of migrant farmworkers, and so many other urgent needs.

It may be a question of leadership. There is the beginning of a Hispanic church leadership, hampered as it may be by the sheer burden of taking up the responsibility to fill the American church's leadership vacuum. But the need for that leadership is there, and the clergy and the Hispanic faithful demand it.

In the recent past, efforts to lead the Hispanic Catholics have wavered between seeking a closer relationship with Latin American churches or considering themselves a specific group within the national American church. At the present time, there seems to be a consensus favoring the latter. Hispanic church leaders claim full membership in the American church, while not abandoning their role as a natural bridge to Latin America. Hispanics are in the American church to stay, as they are in the country to stay. Their growing numbers will continue to give them public attention and political strength. Their own self-confidence will not allow them to be ignored.

In the meantime, will the Hispanic faithful continue to be Catholic, respect the clergy, and honor Our Lady of Guadalupe, San Juan, and *Nuestra Señora de la Caridad del Cobre?*

It is difficult to make predictions. To the extent that racial and ethnic harmony increases in American society, it may also increase between Hispanics and Anglos in the church. Unfortunately there seems to exist today in America a regression and a hardening of social confrontations. The hopes of the '60s calling for a new national commitment to stamp out poverty and racial discrimination have now been given up to a large extent. Economic conditions are of paramount concern. The laws that were passed then seem today a hardly tolerable burden of demands and regulations.

What is more important, there seems to be a fatigue, a sense in many of the most progressive forces in the country that there is not much anybody can do to remedy poverty and prejudice. As a consequence there is a return to an individualistic approach in which those who "don't make it" are blamed for their own failure. Traditional "liberals" are today more concerned with ecological matters and seem to tend toward the exotic. Many that "marched at Selma" now are concerned with the preservation of the whales.

A different sense of fatigue at times overcomes those Hispanics who are at the forefront of Catholic activism in

America. Priests and lay leaders will confess to loneliness in the struggle to bridge the institutional gaps that loom wider instead of narrower every day. Those Hispanics in positions of leadership in the political and social areas have, with a few exceptions, given up and accepted the institutional church as part of the problem, one of the forces that prevent Hispanic social progress. They no longer lead the fight against church policies; there are no demonstrations like the St. Basil Church confrontation of 1969 in Los Angeles. Youths find an identity outside a religious commitment.

Perhaps the future will bring more of the same, and there will be no substantial changes. Family values will continue to be buttressed by religious beliefs. Personal relationships to God and the saints will remain the substance of religion for Mexican Americans, Puerto Ricans, and other Hispanics. And the structured church will stay on the outside of this religious life, looking in and not understanding.

But two factors at least will make this status quo difficult to preserve: on the one hand, the commitment to change and the growing people power of the few priests and Catholic laypeople serving the Hispanic communities; on the other, the determined efforts of other confessions to woo Hispanics, mostly the poorest, to a brand of religion that claims social change as the core of religious involvement. And underscoring these developments is the continuing awareness of the various Hispanic groups in the country. Their level of education is rising, as is, ever so slowly, the economic condition of the people. The American presence of Hispanics will also continue to be reinforced by the population pressures of Latin America.

This trend acquires more relevance in view of the new regionalist forces in America today. The balance of industrial and business power is shifting from the Northeast and the Midwest (the Snowbelt) to the South and Southwest (the Sunbelt), and in the future the move to the energy-rich states in those regions will increase. The two last presidential elections in the country pointed forcefully to that new regional dynamic. The geographical location of Hispanics, heavily concentrated in the Southwest, will put them in a more favorable position to ride the tide of these new developments.

Economic power is already giving rise to demographic strength, translated into political power. The reapportionment of Congress as a result of the 1980 census will transfer power further to the South and Southwest from the North and Midwest. Policies in energy development, taxes, and social programs will increasingly reflect this new geographical balance of American regions.

In a religious-political context, there is also a new mood in the land. It is a new fundamentalism that preaches the total certitude of dogmatic orthodoxy, based however loosely on interpretations of Scripture. This mood, embodied in the 1980 elections in the Moral Majority movement, has militantly embraced the political tenets of the regressive right. It is claiming a major victory in the 1980 elections, and will likely increase that influence in the foreseeable future. Their brand of simple and indisputable statements and beliefs seems to be providing a refuge for those who have grown wary of uncertainty and change.

The Catholic Church is outflanked on the right by the fundamentalists. The fact that it shares convictions with them on specific issues, such as abortion and sex education, is not enough to give credibility to critics who argue that the American Catholic Church also shares with them a regressive social policy posture. The Catholic Church has never explicitly embraced such unconcerned social policies and has a history of teaching that puts it very far from that aspect of fundamentalism.

The American church however faces a challenge. It has a clear progressive message to carry, and that message cannot but be a blueprint for change. The challenge is to bring those teachings to life and for the American church to align itself once more with the poor, the dispossessed, the marginated in the new theological language of the Latin American church.

History is not kind in judging the success of the universal Catholic Church in choosing this alignment over the centuries, and the Latin American church has compiled a particularly unresponsive record in its response to that challenge. But in those countries the church has started to change. The turn has produced its first martyrs, even among priests and bishops.

Nowhere is the challenge more explicit for the American church than in its relations with Hispanics, who are not external to it. There is a growing browning of America, and the Catholic Church must look inward to find the power in itself to join the social revolution that this phenomenon demands. In the process there has to be a browning of the American church—it has already begun.

Hispanics cannot be a "problem" for the American church. They are the way to its future.